CRICKET CHANGED MY LIFE

ELEVEN PERSONAL JOURNEYS

ANNIE CHAVE

First published by Fairfield Books in 2025

fairfield books

Fairfield Books
Bedser Stand
Kia Oval
London
SE11 5SS

Typeset in Garamond and Proxima Nova
Typesetting by Rob Whitehouse

This book is printed on paper certified
by the Forest Stewardship Council

Every effort has been made to trace copyright and any oversight
will be rectified in future editions at the earliest opportunity

The views and opinions expressed in this book are those of the author
and do not necessarily reflect the views of the publishers

ISBN 978-1-915237-51-4

A CIP catalogue record for this book is available from the British Library

Printed by CPI Group (UK) Ltd

CRICKET CHANGED MY LIFE

ELEVEN PERSONAL JOURNEYS

ANNIE CHAVE

fairfield books

To my glorious mam – oh how she'd laugh.

Cricket Changed My Life

Contents

Foreword

YOU WILL ENJOY THIS BOOK. You may also be uplifted by it as a wide range of characters tell Annie Chave why and how the game of cricket has shaped and enhanced their lives. You'll recognise some of the names: David Lloyd, Enid Bakewell, Roland Butcher and Fred Rumsey, four colourful English internationals with stories to tell. Others will be less familiar: Wissal and Maram in Beirut and Waleed Khan from Peshawar have overcome challenges that would seem utterly insurmountable to most of us. Somehow, incredibly, the game of cricket has helped them along the way.

Annie asked me to write this foreword some time ago and I thought then that I might have to introduce her to the wider cricketing public. That's not really necessary now since you'll probably know her already. She is a whirlwind of energy, who has been passionate about cricket since childhood, and she's now a familiar smiling face on the cricket circuit. Her passion is to protect the game she loves. To this end she helped to start a wonderful magazine *County Cricket Matters* in 2019, which has become compulsory reading for those devoted to the county game. Quite a few people may have had the idea of such a noble publication but Annie possesses the tenacity to actually carry the idea through. It requires an enormous amount of hard work as well as creativity and there is an increasing number of envelopes to lick come publication time.

It no longer surprises me that Annie has made a success of this. Such is her enthusiasm and charm that it does not take her long to be in touch with some of the game's legends. I came across her in the Caribbean in 2019 when she first appeared in a press/commentary box and I couldn't help noticing that before the end of the first Test in Barbados she was already having a one-to-one chat with Sir Garfield Sobers. She is not easily intimidated by the big names nor by those who disagree with her, and she has now interviewed many seminal figures in the game. As well as producing the magazine, she has been broadcasting regularly on county cricket for the BBC, writing for a variety of publications including a fortnightly column in *The Cricket Paper*, and contributing behind the scenes to The Cricket Society and the Cricket Writers' Club.

This is her first book and probably not her last. Her knack of getting people to talk is in full blossom here. She herself is a good talker but, even more importantly for this lovely project, she is a good listener too. All her subjects, with their wide varieties of background and experience, have opened up to her with eagerness and candour. And before long we end up thinking this is not such a bad game.

Vic Marks, March 2025

Introduction

I KNOW THE VILLAGES in Devon by two landmarks: the pub and the cricket ground. I grew up as child four in a cricket-mad family, and our summers were shaped around weekends travelling across a patchwork-quilt map of glorious grounds.

From 1975, my dad played for the Exeter University Staff team, the Erratics. He was a decent bowler, a middle-order batter and a very good wicket-keeper, who continued to keep until he was 75, still agile and with fast reactions until, sadly, his eyes began to let him down. The cricket was, of course, incidental for us children. We explored the wilderness beyond the boundary, only aware of the game's progress when we had to wait (impatiently) to wolf down the remains of the tea like an army of ants.

Those times stick fast in my memory as glorious long afternoons that stretched into slow shadows and warm layers. Although we were aware of, and sometimes intrigued by, the cricket, we were content in the knowledge that our parents were there, somewhere, and that while the game lasted, we were irrelevant to them.

It was around the age of nine that I was pulled closer to the boundary. Absorbing myself in the cricket, I began to spend time with my dad – learning how to score – and found that the game on the pitch was completely compelling. Long evenings in pub gardens were equally entertaining. Our outlaw mischief was accompanied by shrieks of laughter from the sets of parents as the beers piled up and the plumes of smoke got thicker and thicker. I remember, on a few occasions, tugging on my mam's arm begging for bedtime, but those were very rare exceptions.

Cricket continued to fill my summers, with both my brothers, my sister, myself and my husband all playing for the Erratics. My brother Jim took it one step further when he organised a tour with his family and friends, assembled as a team under the name of Mystics and Magicians – bafflingly borrowed from Alexandra David-Néel's *With Mystics and Magicians in Tibet*. The Mystics played their inaugural match against the Erratics in 1984 and undertook their first tour (of Ireland) in 1992. Annual jaunts – to Scotland for a decade or so, and now to Cornwall – continue: a group of friends united by the game of cricket. There are few activities that can be similarly sustained.

Introduction

It seems, in retrospect, inevitable that our son should be into cricket. He was born with Test Match Special being played in the delivery room. It was the fourth Test against South Africa, and Angus Fraser was taking five wickets (ten in the match). So it seemed only fair to call him 'Fraser'. While I was in labour, my dad and brothers were playing cricket 100 yards down the road – in the last game ever played (before the University sold it) on the Erratics' home ground.

It so happened that, at the time of Fraser's birth, my dad was batting (for the Erratics against the Mystics). He was informed from the boundary (Jim's wife miming the rocking of a baby) that his first grandchild had arrived, and he was out next ball (caught behind the wicket by his younger son), with sentimental tears obscuring his vision. Fraser was awarded Erratic of the year in the light of this delivery.

Hours of Fraser's childhood were spent at village cricket grounds, watching his father opening the batting, and I couldn't even begin to count the number of times we walked the boundary together watching him bat, Fraser with ball or bat in hand. His childhood echoed mine, and I was happy in the knowledge that it couldn't be a better grounding for him. He has developed into a fine left-hand batter and off-break bowler whose greatest joy has become playing friendly cricket for the Erratics. It was one of my most delightful days on the cricket field when he played alongside my dad, his dad and my brothers. And I was scoring!

I've always loved international and county cricket, too. I've been a supporter of Somerset since, at the age of eight, I saw Viv Richards and Joel Garner playing at the Devon County Ground at the top of our road. I had never seen anything like it. I don't think I ever have since. I was a silent supporter then. Cricket happened in front of me, and I had no voice to sing its praise. And then I joined social media, at a time when it could still unite people rather than divide them.

I found a group of people on Twitter who felt the same way about cricket as I did, and it wasn't long before I became part of the online cricket community. The blog site *Being Outside Cricket* was the first to contact me to ask if I wanted to write an article. I was then invited by *Guerilla Cricket* to join their 'alternative' broadcasting station and to commentate on cricket. That, really, was when I began to find my voice. In an echo of Miles Jupp's *Fibber in the Heat*, where he blags his way into the media centre at an international cricket match, I was asked to go to Barbados in January 2019 to help with the coverage of

England's Test match there. I worked with Vic Marks, Roland Butcher and Tino Best for *Line & Length*, a Caribbean radio station, enabling me to experience life at the top of the game.

Then in November 2019, together with a group of like-minded people on Twitter, I helped to bring out a magazine called *County Cricket Matters*. Its first issue was called 'The 100 Edition'. It featured articles expressing our alarm at the sudden insertion of The Hundred into the domestic calendar and its consequent prominence. In March 2020 I took on the editorship, just as lockdown hit. It seemed to me important that the emphasis should be more on championing county cricket than on combating its rival novelty. The magazine is now in its sixth year. It provides a platform for new and established writers with an interest in county cricket, as well as featuring interviews with some of the summer game's major figures and, of course, a cricket crossword.

It has been my good fortune, in the wake of all this, to be invited to contribute to discussions on radio, television and podcasts, as well as providing the 'third voice' for the BBC at Somerset's home games. I mention all this as a way of illustrating how cricket has, over the last six years, transformed my life. It was my grateful recognition of this that gave rise to the idea of this book.

The people who are the subject of the following chapters have all, in widely varying ways, had their lives shaped, or re-shaped, by cricket, all experienced the unpredictable and often life-enhancing properties of the game.

There are examples of cricket's power to reclaim lives lived on the brink of despair. The Pakistani Waleed Khan was a teenager when he was shot six times in a terrorist attack. How did cricket become the driving force behind his recovery, and how did he become a role-model for many through his motivational speeches and his ability to find positives where others would see only negatives? Bharat Sundaresan is a hugely popular commentator and journalist, based in Australia. He explained to me how he overcame two drug overdoses on the way to the career built around cricket for which he believed himself destined. Enid Bakewell grew up in a Nottinghamshire mining village where her love of cricket was formed, and where she developed her eye-catching skills. She went on to become widely considered England women's best-ever all-rounder. I came to wonder at the way, despite the shocking lack of financial support, facilities or recognition for the women's game, Enid managed to force her way into the 1970 *Wisden*. The accolade of a place in the cricketing Hall of Fame in 2012 was overdue. A unique and fascinating woman, Enid is still playing cricket in her mid-eighties.

David Lloyd (also still playing the odd game!) has lived his life alongside cricket, first as a player, then as a coach, umpire and popular commentator. We talked about his humble upbringing and his long and rich journey to the top of the game. There are fascinating lessons in unexpected places. 'Bumble' represents all the indomitable cricketers who have, against the odds, found success. In an utterly different part of the world, I was blown away by the bravery and determination of Wissal Al-Jaber and Maram Al-Khodir, two girls who, having had to flee from their homes in Syria, now live in a refugee camp in Lebanon. These teenagers, with unfettered enthusiasm flooding their voices, told me how their lives have been transformed by cricket. Their joy in life, in such harsh conditions, is as infectious as it is heart-warming.

Other life-stories that captivated me include that of Roland Butcher, the first black cricketer to play for England, Sue Redfern becoming the first woman to umpire in men's first-class cricket and that of Fred Rumsey, a giant of a man in more than a literal sense, who oversaw the early years of the Professional Cricketers' Association (PCA). Fred would have been as intrigued as I was to meet and talk with Callum Flynn, an England Disability cricketer, who defied his cancer diagnosis at the age of fourteen, or the young journalist Georgie Heath, who has fought a life-threatening eating disorder to become a successful commentator.

Dan Norcross, now a well-known voice on Test Match Special, reached his nirvana by loving the game so much that he created his own broadcasting company.

Readers of this book will encounter a diverse group, whose variety highlights the fact that cricket can benefit anyone, that the game's reach is not confined to its players. Indeed, at times it can be much more. The French painter Georges Braque said: 'Art is a wound turned into light.' Well, cricket can turn the broken into beacons.

Annie Chave, March 2025

Waleed Khan

A LOUD NOISE; deafening bang after deafening bang. A piercing sound cuts through the air and fills your ears, replacing the laughter that a moment ago had rung out across the room like music. A dark stream of blood replaces the wide smile that had lit up your friend's face. He has been shot. Shot in the head. He falls to the ground, one of a growing body count littering the hall.

It's confusion rather than terror that fills you. Minutes ago, you were standing happily on the stage in your school hall with your teachers. Now it is a battlefield as men with guns burst through the doors. "Shoot at their heads," they shout. A cacophony of chaos and screaming, gun shots, frenzied footsteps. Searing pain like you've never known. You've been shot in the face, and you cry out with a mixture of despair and agony. The gunman comes closer, searches your tear-filled eyes. Seeing that you're not dead he shoots you. Again and again. You're hit six times, your jaw spread across your face, your teeth lost, your nose broken, but you are not dead; helpless, but not dead. You are left to die in pain.

In this nightmare, you realise that if you want to stay alive you need to leave the smoke-filled auditorium. Unable to help your dying friends, you manage to crawl out, but you're so weak that you fall, and those fleeing behind you in blind panic trample over your broken body. No one is looking down, only ahead, desperate to escape. You can't speak because your face is an open wound, and your hands and wrists are trampled on and broken in the terror of the moment. You are paralysed with fear and pain.

You are discarded in a pile of the dead and struggle to stay conscious. You can't move, can't talk. You are dimly aware of the emergency services that have replaced the terrorists, and of the true horror unravelling around you. School transformed into war zone. You do everything you can to breathe deeply, blood bubbling in your open mouth, somehow knowing that to stay awake is your only chance, and then you are discovered. You remember nothing more.

* * *

I meet with Waleed in Birmingham in September 2023. He is a delightful and incredibly sincere 21-year-old with fading scars on his face, a battlefield of bruising signalling the atrocities that a young life should never have witnessed. His recovery, he claims, is down to superb medical support, his family, friends, and an intense passion for cricket.

A school should be a haven, and the Army Public School was seen as the best in the Peshawar area of Pakistan, Waleed explains as he begins to relay his story to me: a well-practised monologue of a terrible tale. His parents would have been content knowing their two youngest sons were safely at school. It was 16 December 2014, a normal morning sitting in the café with his friends at breakfast, still basking in the glory of their latest sporting success. The week before, he and his friends had won the inter-school sports competition, winning prizes in table tennis, cricket and basketball. It was a fantastic achievement and they had been greeted with much praise. "We were in celebration mode," he tells me. "We could not stop talking about it."

Waleed, at 12 years old, was not only captain of the cricket team but also one of the school's youngest ever head boys. After breakfast, together with around 500 students aged between 11 and 18, he attended a first aid talk in the main hall. One of the bonuses of being head boy was to be on the stage with the principal and, on this occasion, the army doctor, who was delivering the talk. He was standing up there, between these two men, desperately trying to avoid eye contact with the friend who was trying to make him laugh when gunshots were heard. With an army barracks next door, these were not unusual sounds, so there was no immediate concern inside the huge auditorium, but the reassuring words from the principal were soon silenced as the shooting became closer and louder. So loud.

The teachers' smiles began to fade as they rose to lock the doors, instinctively telling everyone to hide under their chairs. A deathly silence inside; a barrage of bullets outside, released into the bodies of the hapless gardeners. The group of terrorists made their way up the steps to the front of the school and broke through the doors of the hall. 153 people were killed in the brutal attack, 132 of them children. Waleed lost all of his close friends in a matter of moments. Twenty-seven members of his class were killed – every single person except him. His place on the stage meant that he witnessed the full horror of the vicious attack. "I stayed standing where I was on the stage, too confused to move," he says, and the stark reality is that had he been with his friends, he would not have survived.

Not that the stage remained safe for long. Waleed himself soon became a target, and after he had been shot repeatedly it is incredible he managed to move as far as he did. It certainly saved his life. It was only when he was finally found that he lost consciousness. He was rushed straight to hospital, but his chances were slim: 0.5% slim, he was later told. "They told my family that they should not expect me to survive, and the doctors gave them an eight-day cut-off, which meant that if I didn't regain consciousness by then they would not continue to treat me."

Fortunately, on the eighth day Waleed woke from his coma. He had been given another chance, a last-gasp reprieve. His immediate reaction when he woke, he says, was to panic and try to tear the oxygen mask off his face, to free himself from the bed. Terror was still foremost in his mind, and he was petrified if any doctor or any stranger entered his room for days afterwards. His survival was a miracle, and his family worked hard to protect him from the truth of the event, not allowing him to see his own face or to hear all that had happened. "My mother even tried to convince me I'd been in a bicycle accident," he smiles, but he had some recollection, his memory returning like the end of the reel in an old movie. It was when he was finally left alone that he decided he needed to search for the truth. He found the news on the internet. "When I saw it on social media," he tells me, "it was the most devastating thing in my life."

He'd known it was a massive attack. He could remember the noise and the pain, reliving the fear every time he closed his eyes, but learning the whole truth meant he had to come to terms with losing his friends all over again. And then, when he finally saw his face in a mirror, it was another hammer blow. The person looking back at him was so changed. So damaged. "I thought how am I going to face the world now? It took away all of my self-esteem. I had nothing left."

As well as being subjected to long and complicated surgery, Waleed was suffering from post-traumatic stress disorder. He received regular counselling and was carefully supported by his family. Because of the number of operations, the recovery time needed, plus the inevitable mental-health issues, it was two years before he was able to return to education. In the meantime, he needed an outlet. That came in the form of cricket, his great passion, and it helped not only to give him a sense of normality and focus, but also to get him to follow a "yellow brick" pathway that led to some of the best experiences of his life.

It is clear from the way he recounts it that he received very careful treatment, both under the knife and in the counsellor's chair, but the reality was Waleed had just reached his teenage years and needed to lose the victim status that had been stamped onto his face with such cruel scars. Thankfully, early on in his time in hospital, whilst recovering from major surgery both in Pakistan and in England, Waleed had two experiences that had a huge impact on his journey of recovery.

The first was a fairy tale for any fan of cricket. Just before he left for England, the Pakistan cricket team were playing the 2015 Cricket World Cup, and the players all came to visit him in hospital. Among the visitors was Shahid Afridi, who, as Waleed excitedly explains, was and is his ultimate hero. He had followed the Pakistani team avidly since he was a young child, letting cricket rule his moods, as so many sports fans do.

Before the incident, Waleed admits with a shy smile, he attributed many of his happiest and darkest moments to the successes and failures of the Pakistani cricket team, finding it hard to separate their results from the successes and failures of his own life. "Since my childhood I've been really attached to cricket – it was my elder brother who got me watching it from a very early age, and I remember, in 2011, when Pakistan lost the [ODI World Cup] semi-final to India, three days afterwards, when I got my exam results and I'd done very well, I was so miserable that the teachers asked my mum why isn't he happy? And she had to say he's still unhappy about the cricket."

It was an amazing experience for Waleed to meet the Pakistan side, his heroes all there to see him and him alone. It was hard though, he agrees, not to have his friends to share this with. How often, when your dreams meet reality, do you want to reach out to those closest to you and relive the experience with them? But the visit reinforced just how much cricket and those who played it mattered to him, and this served to give renewed purpose to a life that, for the previous year, had been solely focused on recovery and loss.

It took five long and very tough months before his body was sufficiently healed to allow him to travel to Birmingham for the necessary facial reconstruction. His panic had subsided, but it was a very fragile young man who arrived in England six months after the nightmare attack.

His past life was left behind, although the massacre constantly replayed in his memory, his brain still fighting desperately to alter the inevitable ending. The hospital in Birmingham was a sanctuary of sorts, but it was hard to escape the online media story that pursued him. His father left his job in Pakistan to travel with him and stay at his side as he recovered and underwent endless operations.

The second experience took place shortly after he had made the journey to England and was trying to adjust to life in hospital when a stranger, who had heard his story, set about trying to improve his situation through a shared love of cricket. Waleed had just undergone a 12-hour operation which left him even more incapacitated than before. "In order to reconstruct my jaw, they had to take a bone from my leg, which meant I wasn't able to walk. My doctors told me I wouldn't be able to walk without crutches for four to six months. It was quite a hard thing for me, being such a cricket lover."

Shortly after this surgery, Farukh Kazi, the owner of Forward Drive Cricket Academy in Birmingham, a man who claims to eat and sleep cricket, got in touch to ask if there was anything he could do to help him. Farukh has a true generosity of spirit and Waleed is one of many he has invited into his home. Aged 13, having barely left his hospital bed in months, accompanied by his dad, this young boy, leaning heavily on his crutches, must have been overwhelmed by being in a new environment with children his own age again. It's hard to imagine what mental pictures it must have evoked, but the cricket bug is a strong one, and he found himself unable merely to stand by and watch. "It was tough to watch other kids playing and, as they were showing me around, I kept saying I wanted to bowl. Everyone, including my dad, kept saying that I couldn't and that it was too difficult on crutches, but I was so desperate." Eventually, seeing that there was no telling him, they gave him a tennis ball and told him to be careful and not hurt himself. "I was holding my crutches, and I started bowling with the other hand, that's how much I wanted to bowl."

The cricket flame had been reignited, and that meant that he could start identifying as a cricketer, not a victim of terrorism. That identification will never leave him, he's quick to say, but before he could become the inspiration to others that he has become, he needed to find a reason to recover.

"The reason I started walking earlier than expected was when I looked at those kids playing cricket, I had such a longing to do the same. I was there with my crutches, unsteady on my feet after getting out of a bed that I'd been in for such a long, long time, and I didn't want to be there any more. There was a voice inside that was shouting at me 'Join in!'. I wanted to go back on that field and do what I was best at and what I loved the most. Sport does that, it takes you out of yourself."

Over the following months, Farukh treated him as part of his family, and later, when Waleed was able to move without crutches, he allowed him to come and go as often as he needed at the academy, with free access to all the facilities. He went there regularly, working obsessively on his strength and fitness, and getting stronger and stronger, eventually being able to run again, albeit not as fast as before. It was a huge part of his recovery, both physically and mentally, and it meant that, after two years, when he was able to start school he had the confidence and the strength to sign up and get selected for the cricket team. "Cricket is more than just sport," he said in a BBC film about his recovery. "When I'm upset or having those nightmares, it really plays a big role. Cricket is one of the most important things in my life, it really helped me in my rehabilitation process."

As he did in Pakistan, Waleed went on to be the captain of the school team. Despite his obvious injuries he could still bowl at a good pace. "Everyone was shocked when I bowled my first ball and asked me, 'How can you bowl so fast?'" he tells me conspiratorially. He lights up when he talks of cricket. The shy seriousness is replaced by an almost arrogant countenance that is so alien to this self-effacing, quietly spoken young man. It is the self-confidence that comes with ability.

His skill with the ball was such that he was recommended to Warwickshire and he went along for their trials. Unfortunately, the nets coincided with another leg operation, which meant that at the same time as he was starting his recovery, he had temporary post-op problems with his running. "When I went for my trials, it was something I wanted to take forward," he tells me, "but then it struck me that I was going to have more and more surgery, and realistically I would train for maybe three or four months, and then another surgery would be required, and I would need to leave my training for it."

This is a maturity that can only come to someone who has already lived a lifetime of horror and sadness, I think as I digest his words. Most young people would either feel sorry for themselves or think only of a future return to full fitness. Waleed is pragmatic beyond his years and for a while we discuss his 'living for the moment' attitude. He is very assured about this. "One thing that changed in me after this incident is that now I always live in the day. I always feel that if I get through this day, then that's great, it's my achievement."

It's a sobering way of thinking, but I can't deny it is understandable. How do you plan for a future when you've been so close to losing yours? Time spent at the academy helped Waleed to keep focused. He talks a lot in these terms, so adept at using positive language, language he's learned from years of counselling, and years of his own motivational speaking thereafter. It was through the training and the strengthening work he did at the academy – endlessly bowling, endlessly practising – that he felt confident enough to approach two local clubs.

He joined Lyndworth CC and Weoley Hill CC's junior team. This was another step up. "I'm a different person on the cricket pitch." He looks at me as he says this. It's something he doesn't do readily. His eyes, that by some miracle escaped injury in the attack, are so dark and yet so expressive now as he talks about the Waleed he is on the pitch, where he is able once again to be part of a team and thus to travel beyond the hospital boundary, losing himself in the competition on the field.

"When I play cricket, I'm incredibly passionate about it, and sometimes I get really aggressive and competitive too. I get lost in a different world and you see a different me. It was the reason I so wanted to play again. Number one, it was my passion, and number two, I needed desperately to get away from all the negativity that surrounded me. It takes me to another world, one where I don't think about those things and where I'm just engaged in the game. It has helped me so much just by playing a lot of matches. It gives me a sense of freedom and has helped my physical and mental recovery."

Waleed, I suggest to him, needed what he has learned through cricket to gain the confidence, after two years away, to step into a school building and face education again. "Yes, the trauma sticks with you," he admits, "but going back to school was the best decision I made."

He joined the University of Birmingham School, and at first it was tough, tougher than we can imagine, where the educational environment made him relive past horrors. Where noises and strangers made him jump every day. "After weeks of people asking, 'Why do you look like that? Why have you got scars on your face?' I had had enough," he sighs, the frustration clear in his tone of voice.

He decided to do one of the bravest things he could possibly do. Stepping out of the social shadows that he hid in, he asked to stand up on stage and, in front of the whole school, in full detail, he told them what had happened. "I'd become antisocial because of the trauma, and I didn't want to make any friends because I had this fear of losing them again, so doing that was a big step for me. The moment I got up there I started regretting it, I was thinking, what am I going to say to them all? The night before, in my room, I had tried to write it down and so my bedroom floor was full of screwed-up papers. I was worried I wouldn't be able to start, and it was truly terrifying to stand up there, but then, as I was thinking I'd made a terrible mistake, I remembered something my mentor in Pakistan, Muniba Mazari, told me. 'If you're talking to a room of 500 people, you know 499 people won't listen to you, but there will be one person who will be listening to you, and you're there for that one person, to change their life. Don't think of the other people, just think of that one person.' So, I just started talking and talking, and I don't know how long I was there, but I noticed it had become very quiet, and when I looked up, I saw tears in the students' eyes and the teachers were crying. It was the first time someone had got a standing ovation in our school, and that's when I realised my words had so much power because of the story I had to tell. Something that I thought of as my weakness was actually my biggest strength."

Waleed can only nod when I suggest he has now become a celebrity in his school. And it's true, he is now well known across the country for the motivational speeches he has gone on to give. He is keen, he says, to share his story with other young people, and to help them understand how terrorist organisations work, how they try to radicalise people using the umbrella of religion. "I want to show their true face by talking about everything my friends and I went through." Shortly after he gave his school speech, Waleed became one of the early ambassadors for the #Iwill movement, which was started in 2013 by the then Prince Charles. It was set up to give opportunities to young people to express and assert themselves. This is a movement that Waleed fits perfectly, since it gives both support and empowerment for the young "to make a positive difference on issues that affect their lives, their communities and broader society". I can see that it is a movement he clearly loves, and he promotes it brilliantly.

Waleed has also spoken within the cricketing world. In 2019 he was invited to talk at a fundraiser for the Shahid Afridi Foundation. In his naturally self-deprecating way, when we speak of this, he is more excited about sharing a table with the great man than about the fact that he was asked to speak there, but he does admit that it was a great experience. It's hard to imagine that there were many dry eyes in the house.

The emotion was certainly in evident and widespread when, in 2018, he was invited onto Test Match Special during the second day of the England v Pakistan Test Match at Headingley. "I didn't know it was such a big thing before I got there," he admits. During his interview with Jonathan Agnew, as well as talking about the role cricket has played in his recovery, he praised his mother, who gave him strength immediately after he discovered the true horror of the attack. "I was so angry at first," he told Agnew, "but she told me to look positively at the fact I was saved and to get better for my friends." She inspired the idea that it was better to finish this incident with education rather than anger. And Waleed, to the thousands listening, shared a well-rehearsed and deeply felt statement: "With guns and bullets we can only kill a terrorist. With education we can kill terrorism." He may well have made some listeners blush when he claimed that "kids here take the opportunities and the peace in their country for granted." His message was clear. "I've been given the opportunity to change lives," he said. And there is little doubt that he inspired some cricket fans that day.

Again though, Waleed tells me, he was overwhelmed by having so many great cricketers in the box with him. He was so humbled, he smiles, to be in the box with Waqar Younis, Wasim Akram and

Geoffrey Boycott. The view from there, he said, was incredible, and the whole experience surreal. Second only to this was appearing in the same 2019 edition of Wisden as Imran Khan, who had recently become Prime Minister.

"So, you've finished your further education and done your A levels, What now?" I ask. "I always live in the day," he replies, but he does admit to having long-term plans. "I just don't worry too much about them." "So, if it's not cricket, what are the plans?" I ask. The answer, "I want to pursue a career in aerospace," isn't what I expected, but then I ponder. He's obviously a very intelligent young man, he's undergone one of the worst experiences anyone could endure and not only overcome it but made something positive out of it. Why not aerospace? They'd be lucky to have him.

"And cricket?" I ask, and there it is, that twinkle in his eye, that lop-sided smile, that air of authority and confidence. "I have more surgery planned next year," he explains, "but I play when I can." He has a new role now though. "I take my younger brother to the academy to play, he's passionate about cricket. He was still very young when he joined me in England, and he'd see me watching Test or one-day cricket and ask, 'Why are you watching this?' He was only interested in T20s at the time, but the more he watched the more addicted he became, he kept saying, 'This is real cricket,' and he got hooked."

We talk for a while about the limitations of T20 cricket and the joy of Tests. It is hard to exaggerate the sparkle and the change in him as he describes the Tests played on green pitches and the competition between bat and ball. But mostly we talk of a sense of harmony that the game of cricket instils and how, with a good number of overs in the day, Test cricket is, as Waleed says, "the best example of discipline, unity and determination." He wants to help his brother, he says, to experience the joy of cricket, but also to maybe go on and have the professional experience that he couldn't. "He's started playing for his school team and is learning to bowl leg spin. I practise with him as much as I can because I want him to take further what I wasn't able to."

It's significant, and eerily poignant, that his brother is currently the age Waleed was when the attack happened. A perfect age to develop your potential, I suggest. A moment, but just a moment, of silence, while the reality reaches those cautious eyes. "Yesterday," he says with a laugh, "he was home ill from school, and instead of lying in bed he asked if he could go and play cricket, and so Mum grounded him, saying he was supposed to be ill."

Waleed plans to take his brother to Edgbaston as much as he can, both to watch games and to play in the indoor facilities there. He tries to go as much as possible to watch England, but of course Pakistan, and especially the team he grew up with and met, are his passion. He has nothing but praise for Babar Azam, whom he describes as "a game changer". It was when he watched Babar score a hundred live in the World Cup in 2019 at Edgbaston when Pakistan beat New Zealand that he became a huge fan. "Babar Azam can play all formats, he's our Virat Kohli," he beams. It's easy to love the Pakistan team, we agree, and we slip happily into discussing their unpredictability.

And so Waleed, spared death by the barest of margins, will go on to inspire. His motivational speaking and his volunteering work are extremely important to him. No, he won't be the Pakistan cricketer he dreamt of being as a young boy, but he's made a big impact in the world that he inhabits. "The incident has taught me that real happiness is living for others. I don't think I got this second chance without a purpose. It happened and it was terrible, but I have to live with it now and make the best of it. The worst thing I can do is to feel sorry for myself, and I know that because I was in that place for a while, as we're all human, but giving up on something is not helpful. My face lowered my self-esteem to begin with, but the day I accepted myself the way I am was the day I started meeting people, when I started talking and feeling confident and feeling better."

I honestly believe he does feel better, I think as we finish our coffee and I stop recording his voice. How else does a young man who has been a victim of such a traumatic experience agree to meet a stranger in a coffee shop and tell his story to her? A story that involves so much sorrow, so much bravery and so much cricket. It's huge credit to Waleed, and to the careful planning of his family, that he has been able not only to accept leaving his childhood home at such a vulnerable age but also to continue his education and fashion a life in a new country.

"You know to this day I don't know how I managed to survive. I still dream of it sometimes, and even now if I'm walking through the city or there are strangers around I don't feel comfortable, but cricket kick-started the process of surviving, and through that process I have become passionate about campaigning and helping others."

Roland Butcher

STANDING ON THE WHARF bathed in the warmth of a late Caribbean sun, you watch as your mother's boat rocks on the sea swell. You're worried that she will slip, that the emerald water, its white-capped waves dancing around the boarding passengers, will swallow her up. She is leaving you and Margaret, your 10-month-old sister, in Barbados. You know that your father is waiting for her in England. You have no memory of him. You wonder if you will ever see your mother again. As the boat slowly leaves, you stand, your grandmother at your side, waving until it is lost on the horizon. You are three years old.

* * *

Roland Butcher will forever be known as the first black man to play cricket for England. Like Charles Ollivierre, George Headley, Learie Constantine and Frank Worrell before him, his story is written into Black Lives Matter history. It is a legacy that he carries around, as much part of him as his wry sideways smile and the gentle lilt of his voice. There is no bravado in Butcher, no swagger, but he is far more than just his legacy. Today, he works tirelessly to promote sporting activity for all. He's a diligent ambassador for the game of cricket at which he was, in his time, an exciting striker of the ball and an outstandingly agile fielder. He has also been an active and effective coach. In *Rising to the Challenge*, the biography Roland co-wrote with Bridgette Lawrence, his mother is recorded as saying of the little boy she left on the shoreline that he had 'innate sense'. I understand why she said this. Over his career, Roland has shown an inbuilt grasp of what is practical for himself, coupled with a recognition of what is practical for others.

I met Roland when I was working with the Caribbean radio station *Line & Length*, during the West Indies v England Test at the Kensington Oval in Barbados in January 2019. He was commentating with, among others, Vic Marks and Tino Best. (My job was to conduct teatime interviews.) Immediately approachable and welcoming, Roland was soon a good friend and ally. He has since been a regular BBC commentator and I've been lucky enough to meet with him on a number of occasions. This time, I speak to him when he is wintering in Barbados. "I spend half the year in Barbados and the other half in the UK. I have two homes," he tells me, basking in the heat as I feel the bite of a cool October Devon evening. His isn't a bad life, I think. But it's during this conversation that I'm gradually made aware of how Roland is a wonderful mix of both of his homes. His character, it seemed to me, is a perfect blend of two countries.

Roland was born in October 1953 in East Point, part of rural St. Philip, the largest of the eleven parishes of Barbados. His parents were Doreen, a domestic servant, and Robert, a carpenter. It was a tough country in which to start a family, and Robert was soon swept up in the post-war exodus from the West Indies. The British Nationality Act was passed in 1948, and this, together with poor employment prospects at home and a shortage of labour in the UK, led to many in the Caribbean answering the invitation from their 'mother country' to seek a brighter future for their families. Robert left his young family behind in 1955, in the immediate wake of the 'Windrush Generation'.

The Empire Windrush had arrived at Tilbury in 1948, carrying two stowaways and 1,027 passengers, the majority from the Caribbean. Though not the first ship to bring to Britain the immigrant work-force needed there, it was the first to be widely reported. Arriving in 1955, Robert soon found work at the Lyons Corner House in Piccadilly. After he had worked there for a few months, Roland tells me, "Some people came recruiting and my father ended up settling in Stevenage as a boilerman with Kings engineering company."

Doreen was pregnant with their second child, Margaret, when Robert left for England. She stayed with Roland and his sister until Margaret was ten months old, then sailed for England to join Robert in Stevenage, where they were soon married. Roland was brought up by his paternal grandmother. It's a familiar story, we agree. "Yeah, there were quite a few people going to new countries to set up home and leaving the children with grandparents. It was hard enough to live in the Caribbean as it was without having to look after children as well. So it was the norm, really, for grandparents to step into that role," Roland explains. "What was your grandparents' house like?" I ask. "Very, very small. You know, we were a very poor family. It was a typical working-class home. My grandmother was extremely hard-working."

Roland goes on to explain that her employment involved very long hours in the plantation, for which the average wage was around £2 a week. "It was just her. My grandfather had died. She was a strong woman who worked relentlessly." Roland and his sister weren't her only dependents. He tells me that she shared the care of seven grandchildren with one of her daughters. "My Aunt Olga and my grandmother looked after two children belonging to Aunt Olga," Roland explains, "and I had another aunt in England, and she had left her son and daughter, and then another aunt in Canada who had left her son." "No wonder your grandmother had to work a lot," I say. "Yeah, there were quite a lot of us," he agrees. It is immediately obvious that Roland has an unswerving respect for her. He is quick to say that "she never ever complained for a minute. She put everybody before herself."

Life in Barbados for Roland, as it was for many working-class children, was centred around education, farming and religion. His grandmother was extremely strict on finishing homework. It had to be done first. Once it was out of the way, he had numerous outdoor tasks. From the details of these tasks set out in *Rising to the Challenge* it's easy to see the origins of his strong sense of discipline.

In the West Indies you get up very early, six o'clock or before, to start your chores. Every morning, I used to let out the 15 sheep that we had in a pen and take them up to the pasture area. Then I had to tether each of them to an iron stake, because you didn't want them to run away, and I wasn't going to sit there and watch them all day like a shepherd! Once I'd done that I'd go back home and, because in those days we didn't have running water, I would have to go to the local pipe with a bucket to fill the bathtub, making five or six trips over a distance of about half a mile. In addition, we had chickens in the yard that had to be fed and given fresh water. After that I could have my own bath, get changed and go to school.

It didn't finish there, though. Roland had to move the sheep at lunchtime and then bring them home at night. "Then I had to do my homework as quickly as possible so that I could go and play cricket before it got dark." A lot of emphasis was put on the importance of education, and Roland's grandmother ruled her household with fierce efficiency. Barbados, with its warm climate, was ideal for cricket. The weather rarely interrupted what was the favoured sport of the island. Roland, when he was able to get away, would always find a group of friends to play as late into the day as the light allowed. Although his life was full of tasks and duties, he looks on his childhood in Barbados as an idyll of freedom. It was certainly one that he didn't want to leave for a cold home in England, with parents he had little or no memory of. "I didn't want to make the move because I didn't know anything about England," Roland told Bridgette Lawrence. "All I knew was Barbados, where I was quite happy: it was hot, it was nice and I had lots of friends and family there. I was in heaven really; I had no reason to want to leave." Roland describes his life in Barbados as carefree and easy-going, but at the same time very disciplined. It's interesting to see how much that culture has shaped his character.

In 1967, Margaret and a very reluctant Roland left Barbados to join their parents and new siblings in a damp and dreary Stevenage. "How was that?" I ask him, and, in his typically understated way, Roland replies, "To be quite honest, it wasn't something that I liked. England was totally different from Barbados. There was so much more time spent indoors. By that time, we had two more brothers and two more sisters, and so we were adjusting not only to a new country but also a new family." In *Rising to the Challenge*, Roland says a lot about struggling to fit in, admitting he was sullen and unwilling to engage in his mother's attempts to welcome him. He is more circumspect when he discusses it with me. It's not a part of his past he dwells on. Perhaps this is because a lot of time has passed now. A feeling of alienation was almost inevitable: he was in his formative years, and he'd just left behind the person who had raised him since he was a baby. One of the things I noticed about Roland when I first met him was the huge importance he places on his family life. It is present in everything he does and I wonder, as we talk, whether the sense of loss that he must have lived with in his early teenage years is at the heart of his strong family bond.

Rising to the Challenge was published in 1989 when Roland, still playing cricket, was in his mid-thirties. The trauma of leaving his childhood home was still comparatively fresh in his mind. Now turned seventy, he has a wider understanding of the sacrifices that were made to enable all his family to have a more prosperous life. "What sort of house did your parents live in?" I ask, wondering if the move had indeed helped the family finances. "It was quite a big three-storey house, because, by that time, my father had really established himself in the town. And not only that, he also assisted many other family members to come to the UK. One of my aunts who had left her two kids in Barbados – she and her husband were living there, and then an uncle from my mother's side was on another floor." Hearing how Roland's father helped other members of the family to settle in the UK, and thinking he sounds like a generous and extremely responsible man, I find myself thinking, 'Like father like son'.

When Roland and Margaret arrived, Robert was still working for the boiler company, and Doreen, alongside looking after her growing family, did some domestic work in the town. "Do you think they were happy?" I ask him. "Well, listen, as a kid you never know. Obviously, they were both very busy. My father was supporting everyone, even back in Barbados. He was the first to leave and so he was always helping others." I have an immediate image of a big community, like the one Colin Babb describes in his evocative book, *1973 and Me*. Babb describes his childhood in London as part of "a vibrant social gathering of family and friends from across the Caribbean."

His memory is of a cricket-loving community living in each other's pockets. "This included sharing Caribbean food and drink, playing cards and dominoes in a raucous fashion, intrigued by listening to stories about past experiences back in the Caribbean and living in Britain, and opinionated views on politics and cricket in the Caribbean and Britain. All of this was accompanied by a musical backdrop of calypso, funk, Motown, reggae, soca and soul." Roland's Stevenage boyhood, away from the main Caribbean diaspora and a decade earlier than Babb's, was probably quieter. "Basically, in those days, most of the people congregated in London, but we were always completely different because we were in Stevenage. You know, my father was the first black person ever in Stevenage. We were the first black family." "Did they get treated badly?" I ask, automatically visualising the shocked faces of a small town in England. "I don't think he ever did. I mean he's ninety-four and he's still living there." "He's still going then?" I ask, surprised. "Of course, yeah. He's stronger than me. He still has his allotment and grows all of his own vegetables." Roland beams, and I love his slanted smile. "He's in good nick," he continues. "He still has all of his faculties. He built good relationships in the town, and he's well-respected to this day. I don't think he had many hard times." Very personable, like his son, I surmise.

When Roland arrived, there was immediately an issue over his schooling, he tells me. "The nearest school, where my other brothers and sisters went, only had space for one girl. So my sister went there, which meant all five were there, and I had to go to the opposite end of the town, which wasn't the best school to go to. I was one of two black kids in my class. There were five non-white children in the whole school." This won't have helped Roland settle in and feel part of the family. He needed something to reconnect with his Caribbean roots. "And did they play cricket at this school?" I ask, hoping that this would be a route to combat homesickness for him. "No, not really, no. There were a few kids who were interested, and we maybe played about two games a year. Even then we could probably only get about seven players, so that was it." "It was very different from Barbados then?" I offer. "Completely different. It was all about football in England," he replies. And here I come across another side of Roland. He proved to be a very good footballer, the first black player to represent Stevenage, playing semi-professionally. Later, he worked for Arsenal as a football coach in the community. "In those days," he tells me, "cricket was only played from April to September, you didn't play overseas and so I'd play football in the winter months."

Roland might have been tempted to concentrate on football because he was obviously a talented player, but cricket was his first love, and when I ask him how he managed to get back into playing it, although he's a little bit blurry on the details, he explains that "somehow, I got involved with Stevenage Cricket Club, which was close to my home. I started in the third XI and then moved quickly to the second XI and then to the first XI. By the time I was fifteen I was playing for the firsts, as a leg-spinner who could bat."

Roland had found a cricket club, despite the absence of any personal links through family or friends. "Did none of your family play cricket?" I ask him. "Yeah, my uncles did when they were younger, but they were too busy working or looking after families by the time I was playing." There doesn't appear to have been much leisure time for adults, and I get a sense of industry rather than fun from Roland's household, especially when he tells me that, to him, "cricket was an escape from spending so much time indoors." When I ask him if the cricket reminded him of being back home, he's very keen to highlight the contrasting conditions. "It was so different. Everything was different."

And this is true in terms of both societal and playing conditions. In Barbados, the grounds would have been so hard that the ball would fly through to the keeper. In England, the wickets were softer and slower. An ability to adjust to different conditions is the mark of a natural player. I wondered about Roland's own experience. "So, you had to reinvent your cricket then?" I ask. "Well yeah, I guess I was very lucky there because Stevenage had some really good people who looked after me really well." Stevenage had recognised the potential in the young Butcher and helped to prepare him for English conditions. He was beginning to reshape the batting that had been his strength back in Barbados, and at the same time reconnect to that part of his life that he sorely missed.

It was when one of the players in the team, Cyril Hammond, moved from Stevenage to work as supporters' club secretary at Gloucestershire County Cricket Club that things started to change significantly for Roland. "Cyril recommended me to the club as a young player they should have a look at," he tells me. Hammond must have been persuasive as it wasn't long before Gloucestershire invited Roland to Bristol for the summer of 1968, when he wasn't yet fifteen. "You were pretty young," I comment. "I was, yeah," Roland agrees. "I went to Bristol and stayed with Cyril and his wife for the summer and played in the Gloucestershire youth team." The team played cricket every day of the summer. Most of them lived in the dressing-room at the ground. "The coach's wife would come in in the morning and cook breakfast for the boys, and then they would go off and play cricket. At that time there were people like Andy Stovold, David Graveney, Julian Shackleton in the group, and Geoff Howarth was the captain of the youth team."

He was successful enough to be asked back for the summer of 1969. "This time," Roland tells me, "Cyril said, 'I think you need to stay with the boys and get used to that life', and so I lived in the dressing-room. Everything was there for you. You had the sleeping bags, this wonderful breakfast, TV and all the kids together at night doing what kids normally do." This makes me raise my eyebrows. "How was that lifestyle then?" I venture. "It was different and very good, and from the off Andy Stovold and myself became very good friends, so I spent a lot of time with him. He had a scooter, and we'd ride through the villages on it." The image makes me smile; I'm not so sure the villagers did.

Gloucestershire were very happy with Roland's progress, but they thought he was still a little young to join the full-time staff. So it was that, at the end of 1969, they sent him to Lord's for a trial with the MCC. It was something that Gloucestershire would later regret. It led to a misunderstanding that Roland still feels uncomfortable about. "I was an MCC Young Player for 1971 and 1972, with Ian Botham, Ian Gould, Nick Evans and Keith Jennings. Eleven of that group of players went on to play cricket professionally." It was at Lord's that Roland finally realised that he could make a living out of playing cricket. By being part of the MCC team he was ideally placed to be noticed, and he was being noticed. In 1972, when Middlesex offered him a contract, he jumped at the chance. "I didn't really understand the implications behind Gloucestershire sending me to the MCC. I was a bit naïve, and nobody really explained the protocols to me." Gloucestershire were understandably upset that Roland had accepted a contract from Middlesex after they had nurtured him, but Roland, albeit shakily, was following a path that would lead to international honours.

For Roland, there were other benefits to playing for Middlesex at that time. It meant that he was based in London, which was far closer to Stevenage. When I mention this to him, he agrees that its proximity to home was useful. "Stevenage is still over 25 miles from Lord's, but yes, it was closer than Bristol." "And London was a bit more exciting for a young lad?" I ask. But this is Roland, and he isn't fond of big cities, as he's quick to tell me. "Not for me." He smiles. "Don't forget I'm not a bright lights person. I grew up in the country in Barbados. Not a lot happened in Stevenage, but London was a different proposition. During my two years at the MCC most of the guys stayed in digs in London, but I travelled on the train back to Stevenage every day."

"Makes sense," I say, "and it was probably cheaper as well." But Roland's keen memory suggests that it wasn't quite as straightforward as that. "Yeah, I guess it was, but I remember the MCC salary was about £8 per week, and, because I lived more than 25 miles away, they gave me £2 towards my travel, so I was on a top salary of £10 a week. It didn't go very far though, because my weekly train fare from Stevenage to King's Cross was £5.20. Then, I would have to take a train from King's Cross to Baker Street and then a bus from Baker Street to Lord's every day, so really my parents were supporting me." He certainly wasn't earning a fortune.

"When I was at the MCC, it wasn't about the money, it was about ambition. I wanted to be a cricketer, and here I was serving an apprenticeship on how to be one, so that was more important to me. I mean, there were other people in that group who left because the money wasn't enough, but it was never about the money for me." Roland, in his own words, captures the fundamental point. He needed cricket.

There is a striking passage in *Rising to the Challenge* that reveals the important part Roland's Caribbean upbringing played in setting him on the path to professional cricket and instilling in him the drive necessary to succeed. The self-discipline and the competitiveness that were fundamental to his Barbadian beginnings helped sustain him at a high level.

I consciously tried to maintain the standards that I had grown up with in the West Indies. Even in the early seventies, I was still struggling to adjust to my changed environment, and the only thing that I could still identify with from the West Indies was cricket. For me, cricket reminded me of my childhood in Barbados.

The psychoanalyst in Mike Brearley had, I suspect, a field day with Roland. Theirs was a fruitful relationship partly because Brearley was quick to spot what made Roland tick.

Playing professionally for the MCC, Roland had achieved his desire of playing cricket for a living. Moving from the MCC to Middlesex seemed like a natural progression, and he joined a team that was on the up. "Mike Brearley was your captain at that time," I say as a statement more than a question, and Roland makes an interesting point in reply, one that enables him to highlight the comparative short-termism of cricket today. "Yeah, Mike Brearley and Mike Gatting were the only two captains I played under, which is a bit different to today. You know, if you go into the Middlesex dressing-rooms these days, they list all the captains. I found it very interesting that, between 1971 and 1996, Middlesex had only two full-time captains in Brearley and Gatting. But in the period between 1995 and 2024, they had gone through something like ten times that number." This surprises me. I knew it was a lot, but that seems such an extreme difference. It identifies a lack of consistency which, as Roland suggests, "generates a lack of stability. It is little wonder that they have been struggling for the last twenty-five years," he comments. The difference may owe as much to the calibre of those captains and the team that played under them as it does to the effect on cricket of high finance and market values.

In 1976, Roland met his future wife, Cheryl Hurley, a young Barbadian who had recently moved down from Liverpool to London in search of a fresh start. The marriage has survived the test of time and produced two children, Paul and Michelle. A focus on family, which began in Stevenage, remains central in Roland's life. He is, it seems to me, a laid-back and private man, whereas Cheryl impressed me as an outgoing, no-nonsense livewire. Theirs is a solid partnership. From the beginning, Cheryl felt Roland's pain, celebrated his successes and supported him through the tough times. And there were certainly tough times during the early part of his Middlesex career.

In *Rising to the Challenge*, there is a chapter entitled 'The Lost Years: 1974-78'. In it, Roland spells out to Bridgette Lawrence his struggles with form. Looking back, he recognises that, through paying too much heed to others and stifling his natural game, he wasted several years in the attempt to turn himself into someone else. "It wasn't until many years later that I realised that I had been misguided and that my efforts to develop a more defensive style of play had had a detrimental effect on my game. I am an instinctive, natural player."

By trying to convert the player he was into a player he wasn't, he had completely messed with his game. During this period, Roland moved back and forth from seconds to firsts, with flurries of form followed by a series of low scores. He was consistently inconsistent. The true magic of his stroke-play was seen only in glimpses, when his Caribbean freedom enabled him to loosen his arms and play as he used to. It's notable that, despite these fluctuations, Roland had the backing of his captain, Mike Brearley. As he emerged from his stuttering start with Middlesex, Brearley placed confidence in him and confided in him. In 1980, when Middlesex won the Championship, Brearley would often turn to Roland, his fellow slip, for his opinion. He rated Roland highly, aware of his astute cricketing brain.

It was during the more successful season of 1980 that England came knocking. "Was there ever a point where you thought you'd prefer to be playing for the West Indies?" I've always wanted to ask this question, assuming that it would be a dilemma. "No," he answers emphatically. "I mean, probably when I was a kid in Barbados, when I was twelve, but by 1980 I was a grown man with a family, and England was my home. It was my future, and there was never any doubt in my mind." And of course, it wasn't just the international game. There was Middlesex to consider. "There would also be another complication if I did, because I would have made myself an overseas player, which limits the opportunities to play. So that wouldn't have made sense. It wouldn't have been a good thing for my family for sure." In other words, playing for England would safeguard his county career.

Roland received international recognition when he was chosen to play in the ODI series against Australia in 1980. He made an impressive half-century on debut and was subsequently included in the England squad that toured the West Indies in 1980-81. He made his Test debut, appropriately, in Bridgetown, Barbados. Cheryl remembered it well in *Rising to the Challenge*:

It was an incredible feeling watching him come out of the pavilion to go in to bat for England for the first time in a Test match. I remember him walking to the crease and some chap came over and hugged him; there was a standing ovation. I thought they would be totally against him, but the reception was completely the opposite. They did not care who he played for, he was a Barbadian, one of them, and they recognised the achievement for what it was.

Sadly, it was an inauspicious Test debut. Roland was caught by Viv Richards off Colin Croft for 17 in his first innings and lbw to Richards for 2 off 29 balls in his second. England lost the match by 298 runs and the series 2-0. It was a fearsome West Indian side, and Roland was unlucky to have played his only Tests against them. But by the very fact of playing international cricket for England, he had paved the way for others to tread.

"When you got called up to England did you have a sense of the importance of being the first black player to play for England?" I ask, but I already know what his answer will be. "When I got selected, that was never in my mind. It was not something that I thought about. I was just really elated to achieve something that I'd dreamt about, something that I'd wanted to do all my life, and I wanted to try and do my best." Roland doesn't wear his heart on his sleeve, but even he is quite emotional when he says this, and I feel able to ask him if, in the light of Black Lives Matter, he is proud of what he did and what he began. "Yeah, I did start something because since me, there've probably been about twenty-five to take inspiration from my selection. They felt that if I could do it then they could, and it gave them the motivation to work harder and achieve their goals. And so, looking back it was a pivotal moment in English cricket, just not something that I thought about at the time."

Roland did not play for England again after the West Indies tour. That was a big disappointment. He acknowledges he had hoped to have done better and for the team to succeed and he tells me that he thought that, although he'd not done any worse than any of the younger players, he hadn't shone. "But playing for England and being the first black player is an achievement that I'm very proud of, and there's no higher honour." It's clear from the view quoted in *Rising to the Challenge* that Cheryl is more sceptical than her husband about the role of England's Test selectors: 'I am sure that if Roland had been Gatting, Gower or Botham, they would have given him another chance. They had wanted Roland to be a West Indian team all on his own and take on the opposition and when he failed to live up to that billing, he lost his place.'

There may well be some truth in Cheryl's diagnosis, but Roland's cricket wasn't harmed by the selectors' decision. After spending the winter of 1981 playing for the Young Men's Professional Club in the West Indies, he had a successful 1982 with Middlesex, passing 1,000 runs in a season for the first time. This was followed, in 1982-83, by an engagement, in the Australian Sheffield Shield, with Tasmania, where he was joined by the family after Cheryl had given birth to their second child, Michelle.

Roland and Middlesex started the 1983 season positively, but a serious injury in July put paid to Roland's exceptional spell and abruptly ended his season. Middlesex had just reached the final of the Benson & Hedges Cup. On the Monday before the final, Roland was facing Leicestershire's West Indian fast bowler, George Ferris, when he misjudged a bouncer which took the edge before hitting him just below his left eye. That injury, Roland tells me, "not only threatened my eyesight, but also put an end to that successful spell." He underwent two operations as well as extreme pain, and, after two weeks in hospital, went home to be nursed by Cheryl. The post-hospital recovery period was tough for both: "I'd broken all the bones in the left side of my face, and I just had to wait for them to heal. I could hardly walk without it hurting. It must have been awful for Cheryl, as I wasn't the most patient." Roland's frustration over not being able to play cricket and his consequent moodiness must have put a severe strain on their marriage. Fortunately, they both had the good sense to know that the period would end. And it did.

Roland recovered, although his eyesight has never been quite the same. Amazingly, 1984 was his most successful season for Middlesex as he scored 1,251 runs in the Championship. A final highlight of his first-class career followed in 1988, when he stood in for Mike Gatting – absent on Test duty – as captain of Middlesex. He was the obvious candidate. Not only had he been at Middlesex for nearly twenty years, but also his acute knowledge of the game had been recognised years before by Mike Brearley. As Roland says, "I studied the game; I didn't just play it."

Roland is a deep thinker. He knows that, for most black youngsters, it is still not easy to be successful in a sustained sporting career, nor to find satisfying work when playing days are over. After retiring in 1990, he himself briefly pursued a career in coaching football, harking back to his youth in Stevenage. He surprises me with his insight into 'the beautiful game'. "I played a lot of football. Stevenage, then at Arsenal I was a soccer school coach, and I played many years for their ex-professional celebrity team. That was what I did in the winters. I did all my coaching qualifications. I'm a UEFA-licensed coach. I also did ten years at Westminster School as the football and cricket coach. After cricket, I wanted to work in football professionally, and I did for a while, with Brendan Rodgers. He'd just been appointed as Academy Director at Reading, and he asked me to come and work with him. I went to Reading and I ran my own academy team, but I soon realised how hard it was to become a professional football coach. Even with all my experience, I found it so difficult to move on."

"So, is it harder for black people in football?" I ask, and Roland replies. "Far harder. I mean, John Barnes, you know, he comes off the top of the tree, he's a Liverpool and England legend, but he struggled to get an opportunity. I think if Brendon had still been at Reading, I might have stayed and won the good fight, but the fact that he left, and I no longer had him in my corner, made me decide to return to cricket."

Roland left football and went off to be national coach of Bermuda in 2000. Returning to the UK in 2001 he took up a coaching position at St. Edward's School in Oxford. In 2004 he was appointed director of sports at the University of the West Indies (Barbados campus), which was where he was when I met him in 2019. Since then he has worked tirelessly (and it really has demanded tirelessness) in a number of roles, including BBC commentary for his much-loved county game.

In December 2022, he was appointed to the selection panels for the West Indies' men's senior and youth teams. He promotes youth and women's cricket and, in 2023, toured the UK talking about diversity and the ethos of Black Lives Matter, but he's keen to point out to me that "it's not just about black rights. It's diversity, it's gender, it's everything. It's something that I'm passionate about, that people of whatever religion, whatever race, whatever colour, whatever gender should have equal opportunities. I just want equal opportunity."

It's the most passionate I've heard Roland, and I know he's talking from the heart because I've seen just how hard he works, just how much he travels, how much he is willing to share his insight with all. He is a whirlwind of wisdom. I suspect he knows that football was always at best a sidetrack. As he told Bridgette Lawrence, 'It has always been just cricket, cricket, cricket for me. I have such a deep love of the game that I have never really thought about anything else.' I wonder if he knew just how much he would give back to the game, just how important he would be, just how important he is.

Georgie Heath

GEORGIE HAS CLIMBED MOUNTAINS. She has swum oceans. She has fought lions. At least to me she has. And she has emerged the wounded victor. She's a ball of anxieties, wrapped up in a hard shell of supreme confidence. She's a contradiction, a mixed metaphor. Above all, though, she is the product of our broken world.

I first became aware of Georgie on social media, where she is open and honest, laying out her life struggles for all to see. This is new-world bravery, part of a sharing culture that those of us born in another era might find brazen. In fact, it's far from that. It's cathartic and refreshing, and it inspires others to be open about their own mental-health issues. Georgie has become a role model for many.

Marcus Trescothick, in his autobiograpy *Coming Back to Me*, does the same for fellow cricketers with mental health problems. Like Trescothick, Georgie isn't the product of a tough childhood. In fact she comes from a relatively privileged background, both financially and in terms of the healthy relationship she has with her family. She is outwardly confident and obviously very bright. In many ways, she appears to fall into the modern category of 'driven', but the narrative of her life story has been, like Trescothick's, partly shaped by a form of separation anxiety.

I talk with Georgie in the early part of 2024. She is going through a spell of freelance unemployment, which means that, luckily for me, she has time to talk. Our Zoom encounter begins with reflections on the long winter and how much we are looking forward to the cricket season. It's kind of an unwritten rule that cricket journalists tell each other to winter well. We rarely do.

"Why cricket?" I ask first up. "My mum's from Yorkshire, so that's kind of the first tick for cricket in your life. She's named after – and I feel like disowning her every Ashes – Lindsay Hassett, who's an Australian cricketer. Cricket is so much part of her life that she was listening to TMS while my brother was being born. Which is quite funny. It was an England v West Indies series in August 1991." I can immediately relate to this, as I did the same thing when my son was born in 1998. I was excited to come across in Georgie's mother, a like-minded soul. "So, life's kind of always been about cricket, and we'd always go up to Yorkshire from Milton Keynes in the summer," Georgie continues. "There was a lot of beach cricket. You know, if it goes in the sea, you're out, that kind of thing. So it's just always been there or thereabouts."

It's a familiar story, one I've heard from lots of people. It's nice, though, to hear it from a female perspective. "I remember – I must have been about seven or eight – when I was meant to get a bus back from school, and my mum had phoned the school to tell me not to get the bus. 'There's nothing wrong, just don't get the bus.' And I was like, 'What the hell?' Anyway, she was taking us to the cricket. She just didn't want to tell us on the phone. So, after school we went off to watch Northants play at Campbell Park in Milton Keynes. It's beautiful there, with undulating grass banks." I imagine Georgie and her brother as wide-eyed, bohemian kids, bare-footed and running free at the cricket. "We queued for the Old Trafford Test for the 2005 Ashes." She tells me. "We were part of the however many thousand that got turned away, having got up at 3 o'clock in the morning, bearing in mind we live near Milton Keynes. But that's the kind of dedication level."

Georgie is from a sporting family. "I used to do quite a lot of cricket at junior level. And my brother played a lot at school. He was at Bedford, a few years below Alastair Cook." "Did your dad like cricket?" "Yes, but not to the extent of the rest of us; and Mum has always been the one we've done everything with. Dad was a rugby player." So yes, a very sporty family.

It was when Georgie left home that the first warning bells could be heard. "I went off to boarding school when I was 11. And I was the most homesick person you've ever met. I cried so much that a blood vessel in my eye burst." It is a tricky age to leave home for any length of time, but a burst blood vessel in the eye sounds like an extreme reaction, I suggest. "I used to wake up mega-early and just be like full of anxiety because I was at boarding school." Georgie had to get special permission from the headmistress to read copies of *Spin* magazine when she woke early. I must have looked puzzled by this, because she goes on to explain, "We weren't allowed to read magazines because they didn't want us reading the trashy ones at that age. But I was allowed to get up and go and sit on the sofa and read if I couldn't get back to sleep when I woke early and was upset. I read *Spin* and kept up to date with all the cricket. I knew all the rankings and I used to get so annoyed when Jacques Kallis was above Andrew Flintoff in the all-rounder charts." An annoyance I doubt she shared with her peers.

I ask the obvious question. "Why did you go to boarding school if it made you feel so bad?" "I'm pretty academic, very sporty. The school did Music and Drama, and you could do everything, so I really wanted to go. I just didn't realise quite how homesick I was going to be when I got there," she explains, "but once I settled in, I absolutely loved it. Although we didn't play cricket at school, which kind of sucked and didn't help my homesickness." A one-woman whirlwind, Georgie did try to get the school interested. "I told everyone in PE that we were going to have a quick session and I found some old pads somewhere and a random bat, and then I was trying to teach the rest of my PE class how to play cricket on the lacrosse pitch." The main worry, it appeared, was trying not to hit it through the headmistress's window. There are elements of Enid Blyton's *Malory Towers* in this description, and I am thrown back to my childhood, when we all read the thrilling mid-century tales of girls at boarding school.

Considering how tough she found it to cope with being away from home, it's slightly surprising to hear that Georgie followed up her schooling with a gap year in Australia. It's not beyond the bounds of possibility that her boarding experiences provided her with the coping mechanisms to deal with her anxieties. Whatever the reason, she was able to enjoy her trip. She even fitted in watching a 5-0 drubbing in the 2013-14 Ashes. "I'm sure dealing with the Aussies' sarcasm must have been harder than coping with homesickness," I offer, remembering my own experience of the ribbing I received in June and July 1993, when I was working in Australia, and England were being beaten 4-1 back home.

Georgie returned to England for September 2014 to study Psychology at Bristol University. She had always been fit but it was during her time at university that she started to fall into the habits that would lead her to be admitted to a hospital eating unit in January 2018. "When I was at university I had some kind of stomach thing, and then I just had a really poorly tummy for a while, and somehow it slipped from actually being genuinely ill to just continuing in the same vein. But people kept saying, 'Oh, you look great. You've lost some weight', and then you're, like, 'Cool, that wasn't the original intention, but I'm happy with the result.' And then it carried on and on. And the bar just gets lower and lower, and there's never an end-line, you know. You just keep moving the goal-posts. And the last goal-post is a grave, I guess. Which is awful and terribly morbid."

By the time she left university, Georgie admits that she was very ill indeed. She explains that it had gradually got worse over the three years, but "it had never manifested as badly. I lost loads of weight as I was coming to the end of my course. And then, if it went in, it came out basically." Her head, it seemed, had taken over her body. Georgie refused to put anything into her body: no water, no paracetamol, no vitamins. She tells me that she refused to take anything that was going to do her any good. It's a stark warning to anyone and highlights just how easy it can be to fall into a pattern of behaviour that can spiral out of control.

Your mental state is often stronger than your physical one. She was, as it turns out, only moments away from harming herself irreparably. "The day I arrived at hospital," she says, "they told me that if I had come 24 hours later, I would have been dead because I was damaging my organs so badly. By that point I had had two heart attacks and suffered liver damage and partial heart failure."

I try to digest the information by attempting to get her weight-loss into perspective. I ask her how many kilos she had got down to. "Bearing in mind I'm 6 foot tall, I was 36 kilos. Which is less than my mum's dog weighs," she replies. "I couldn't roll over in bed without thinking I was going to pass out." She paints a vivid picture, and it's not a pretty one. "What year was this?" I ask. "2017, like two days before Christmas." Doctors were sufficiently concerned about Georgie's condition to have her sent to a consultant for assessment where, she was weighed and measured. "My consultant was only 4' 9", and she had to try and measure me, and even though I'd got to the point when I could barely even register my own name, I got the giggles when she had to go and find a table to stand on to be able to reach the top of my head."

Georgie was told to come to the eating unit in two weeks. "They only have fifteen beds, so basically you are looked at to see if you are sick enough to deserve one. They were like, 'Right you can come in in January,' which was a couple of weeks later. So, in that time, my brain's thinking, 'In two weeks' time, they're going to force-feed me. So, let's make myself as ill as I possibly can in this time.' And that was a terrible two weeks. I don't know how it didn't completely destroy my relationship with my mum." I can only imagine how tough it must have been for her mum, battling with her seriously sick child at Christmas, trying to make her eat something when Georgie was determined to starve herself. She took Georgie to a few different therapists: "One of them had decided that I didn't have an eating disorder. I had a stomach problem that meant I should eat a teaspoon of something every two hours. And she's this qualified therapist being like, 'Eat a teaspoon of peanut butter every two hours and you'll be all right and start gaining weight.' She will never be in Mum's good books!"

Georgie explains that by the time she went to the eating unit in January 2018, she was so ill that she got out of the car, walked into the building and passed out. And she has no memory of it. "I used to pass out quite a lot, because I had really low blood pressure and potassium. I once fainted in a petrol station, and there was no one around, so I woke up and was like, 'Where the hell am I?' I still have the lump on my head." This time, though, she was close to death and they put her in a wheelchair and took her straight to the Leicester Royal Infirmary. "They had to ring Mum and tell her that I wasn't actually in their hospital because I had nearly died. I was there for five nights, and I don't think there was a part of me that wasn't attached to a drip."

During that time the main thing that Georgie remembers is that her brain was completely scrambled. She'd been put in a dementia ward, and the person in the bed next to her died on her first night, which she found hugely stressful, especially in her confused state. The saving grace, she tells me, was that an Ashes Test was taking place that week. "I'm in a hospital where you're awake through the night and all you can hear is dementia patients yelling this, that and the other. And I literally spent the entire time with the Ashes in my ears, basically to try and keep myself sane. I didn't care how we were doing. I probably couldn't tell you what was happening because I had no brain capacity. But the whole time I had a pair of headphones on so I didn't have to listen to anything else, didn't have to hear the beeping. And then, when it finished, I'd rewind it to the beginning and listen to the whole session again, because it was the only thing that kept me going."

It's a common theme I've found in many of the people I interview. Immersing yourself in watching or listening to cricket can be a healing process, a solace. In this case, it kept Georgie from the depths of despair. "I don't know how I would have stayed sane during those five days without it, because it was literally just me. I couldn't read, couldn't do a crossword and there was nothing else I could do in my life other than go to sleep and then try and attempt the awful task of eating my food. The cricket kept me going."

For the next four months Georgie's home was the eating unit in Leicester. "Fifteen of us, one boy and nobody above the age of sixty. The oldest lady used to walk round and round the whole building, which you're obviously not allowed to do. But she would just do it. It's not like they could stop her." "Were you on a drip then as well?" I ask. "No, but you had to pee in a commode so they could check your bladder. I refused to poop in it though, because that's just disgusting." "Did you form any friendships?" I ask, trying to understand whether there would be any kind of bond between members of a group of people placed in such an artificial situation. "There was one girl there who I got along really well with. We became good friends and kept each other going, but she passed away just over a year ago. She'd been in and out of there a few times, having had a horrendous time with her dad when she was younger, and that had just messed her up, basically." This not uncommon story for eating disorders leaves me wondering about the various narratives that brought Georgie's fellow sufferers to their crises, and what happened to them after they left the unit.

For Georgie, there is a sporting lifeline that enables her still to smile. "There was one doctor in there who really liked sport too. I used to talk to him about what sports were going on. He was a big Leicester Tigers fan but loved his cricket as well. We used to get along really well, which was quite nice." Sport, she explains, also provided something to aim at. "I knew that if I got out, I'd be able to actually go and watch the cricket again. And I kept thinking that if I am ever in Leicester again, it'll be for cricket rather than to go to Glenfield Hospital." This mindset kept her going through this bleak time and provided her with a determined resilience.

"Did they have a weight target for you to reach?" I tentatively ask. "No, it was very weird. Some people got sectioned, and they would have to be taken off a section before there was even a consideration of them leaving. With other people it involved a discussion with the doctor, because it was complicated. Your weight can be restored, but your brain can almost get worse. Your body looks how you don't want it to look, but to other people you look healthy when, in fact, your brain is way worse. So it's quite hard to judge."

It's when she goes on to explain the weighing process that my mind is taken to Ken Kesey's *One Flew over the Cuckoo's Nest*. "We used to get weighed on Tuesday morning and Saturday morning. We'd all queue up in our pyjamas. And they'd say things like, 'Great, you've gained 1.2 kilos in the space of three days, now go and eat some breakfast,' which is the last thing you want to do." "And was it tough to eat?" I ask, knowing the answer. "Yes. And I think it's almost worse to be in one of those places, because you observe each other, and then you sort of pick up different habits. The way they did it for us, there were three different tables for patients at different levels. When you first go in, because you can't just suddenly start eating loads and you need to have a certain number of calories per day that are measured out for you, you're placed at table one. There's a ratio of one staff to one patient on table one, and then, at table two, there are just two staff for all the patients. Then, on table three, you don't have any staff at all, and you have your own jams and spreads rather than the exact quantity. The patients there are the people closest to leaving, basically."

Maybe it's the easy way she talks about life and death, but I find this really quite stark. It feels as if she is describing the enactment by a group of adults on the percentile charts familiar to mothers of new-born babies, with those on table one only just alive. The starkness shifts towards the grotesque as Georgie explains the post-breakfast routine. "You have a certain amount of time to eat your meal, and then you all go and sit in the living room together for another forty minutes. The bathrooms are locked for that time, and you are given a wristband that buzzes when your food has gone down enough, and then you're allowed into the bathroom. So we'd all basically sit there for forty minutes trying to pretend we really enjoyed eating that meal. 'Yay, we love food, so great.'"

I try to make sense of it. A group of people who don't want to eat sit in a room together and pretend that they do. It feels so old-fashioned. I think of Kesey's Chief Bromden pretending to be mute and deaf. Georgie continues with her dark description: "And if someone didn't finish their meal, we would then all have a meeting to sit down and support this person. And actually, it was just bollocks, because they were asking us how do we help her? But we're not trained to support, and it's almost like a punishment for them, but not quite a punishment. Even now, when I think about it, I still think it's such a weird concept, because in my head I'd be thinking, 'Well done. I'm so jealous that you didn't eat your meal.'"

Georgie served her time, and admits that she was 57 kilos when she left the eating unit. So they had done their job and helped to save her life, but it just seems like such a traumatising way of doing it. She went back to her mum's in Milton Keynes, but continued as a day patient. This involved her driving back to Leicester twice a week to have lunch and be weighed. After that, she lived near her mum and had twice-weekly visits from her.

"Did they give her strict instructions on what to feed you?" I ask, a bit confused by the abruptness in the change in treatment going from such careful monitoring to being left almost entirely on your own. "No, they give you a meal plan, but you're sent out into the community, and I had Milton Keynes eating-disorder unit, which I think is shut down now. And I know this sounds awful, but the woman that I had to go and see was severely overweight, which doesn't help. I'm just looking at this woman who is telling me to gain weight, and thinking, you're probably more ill than I am right now."

Georgie was still under 18 BMI, which, she explains, is still considered severely underweight, but you are deemed able to function normally in society. She tells me that, "If you're under 15 BMI, then you are not allowed to drive or to fly." She wasn't far from this point, but for the moment she was free from the eating unit, although it wasn't plain sailing, she admits. "I was doing better and then started getting worse again without really realising. I had to have two wisdom teeth out, and it didn't go very well, so I couldn't eat very much and then my brain was telling me, 'It's cool that you can't eat anything,' and so I started losing weight again, which meant I was back talking to the community people in Milton Keynes."

Despite this, she had managed to go back to CCTV, an outside broadcast company, where she had begun doing some work for after leaving university. They had kept her role open through her long spell in hospital. "I went back there two days a week, but I really didn't want to work in an office. I'd come out of hospital and felt the need to do something with my life, and I wanted to go into sports journalism. So I applied for a diploma that I could do part-time. It was timetabled for Tuesday nights and all-day Saturday, including a Sports module that was on a Friday for six weeks. And I got accepted."

"And you were fit enough at this point?" I ask, impressed that she had the room in her brain for studying. In her view, it was essential for her recovery, as she makes clear when telling me about her fight with the women at the Milton Keynes unit. "Yes, I needed to go in a direction. I knew I wasn't going to use my Psychology degree, and this course gave me some purpose and motivation." Georgie admits that she was still feeling low, and her weight wasn't improving. "I was having to go and see the team in Milton Keynes, who kept telling me that I should stop doing my course and spend all of my time focusing on my recovery. And it's like, 'So I should sit at home and just let my whole brain think about eating? That's stupid, and it's not happening.'"

The disagreement continued until both parties decided it wasn't working between them. They agreed it was pointless for Georgie to come every week just to argue, and they arranged to have their last session the following week. "Me and Mum turned up and there were two of the women, this random student woman who I didn't know and these two male doctors. The woman came straight to the point and said to my mum's face, 'We're going to section Georgie today'. And Mum said, 'What? No, what are you on about?' We then had to talk to them for over two hours, and I basically had to sit there and fight my corner as to why I shouldn't be sectioned."

Georgie had got to a point in her life where, in order to recover, she needed a focus, and that focus was her future. She fought to safeguard it. "My weight wasn't enough in their eyes, but I was getting on with my life, pushing my weight loss aside and functioning." "How did you convince them?" I ask. "Well, I honestly can't remember what I said, but apparently I spoke quite eloquently, and it worked because at the end they decided they weren't going to section me, but that I needed to do X, Y and Z and continue to see them." Georgie was adamant that she was not quitting her course. "I didn't care what they said or tried to do. I wanted to do this."

She was determined, and she completed her studies successfully, making some good friends in the process. It was through the course, and through the job-opportunity emails that they sent out to their students, that Georgie noticed there was a cricket writer's competition in connection with the 2019 World Cup. She was revising for her exams and so had the time and chance to enter it. She was the only girl, and most of the others were covering football, and they all encouraged her to go for it. "There were about 100 of us that turned up. We had to go to Trent Bridge and watch a press conference with Mitchell Santner. Straight afterwards we had to write a match report, a sort of colour piece. I did that and didn't really think any more about it because there were so many people, I didn't have a chance. And then, amazingly, I got through to the final three, which meant that I got to go to Edgbaston for the semi-final, England versus Australia, which obviously we won. I had to write a match report from that game and they said, 'We'll let you know'." It's a far cry from an eating unit and from arguing your corner. It's more like the golden ticket in *Charlie and the Chocolate Factory*.

"You know what happens from here?" Georgie asks, "I was so excited every time my phone buzzed for the next week, my anxiety levels were sky high. And then I got a message to say that I'd won. They asked me to do a report for the final on 14 July. And it was just like the best day ever. It was my mum's birthday, and she had to drive me to Lord's from home because the trains weren't running. She was so determined that I would get there. I wrote up the final, got to go to the post-match press conference and everything. It was a brilliant day."

At the same time Georgie had found a job to apply for, with an interview the next morning. "Well, obviously I had no voice whatsoever for the interview, but I got the job. It was with this start-up women's sport company." Everything was falling into place, and Georgie is clear that this came about through the "determination of knowing what I wanted to do, and ignoring the women at the Milton Keynes eating unit. I told them that I was going to finish this diploma and that I was not postponing it. If I had, then I wouldn't have entered the writing competition. I got a job, and I've since been able to say that I wrote for the ICC as one of my first ever published pieces." "And during this time your weight was OK?" I enquire curiously. "Yeah, I mean, it was like up and down. To me, I looked much better, and I was with people who'd never seen what I probably should look like. But my brain was working well, or I wouldn't have been able to do my exams, write all these pieces and travel to and from London doing stuff. There was a point in the middle of that year when I did have a full-on panic attack, like a proper melt-down. And there was a day when I basically nearly walked in front of a bus. I kept crossing this road and I can still remember it now. I almost felt sick. I was going to do it, and then the only thing that stopped me was because it was February, and I hate being cold and I thought if it didn't work I'd just be lying in the cold and that would suck."

It's odd for me to hear life talked about so cheaply, but I recognise that it's part of the illness, a kind of skewed determination that defies logic. "So you obviously suffer with anxiety still?" I ask. "Yeah, and I've had, you know, depression, anxiety, all of the above. I've tried all the different pills before and got to the point I was like, 'None of you are doing anything for me,' so there felt no reason to be on them. They were just numbing me. I'd rather have a cry and be able to feel something, even negative, than feel nothing. I remember being at my grandpa's funeral and thinking I really should be crying, but I actually didn't feel anything right then."

When you meet Georgie she is so lively, and she oozes confidence and competence that it's hard to imagine the dark thoughts and the inner demons that she battles with daily. I ask her whether she is still freelance, and her answer prompts me to worry whether it is the best way for her to be employed, given the anxieties that lurk beneath her surface. "Yes. I'm currently very unemployed and in need of some work, because when I'm unoccupied then my brain starts going into overdrive. When I'm working, I love it, and I get to travel to different places. I do a lot with women's cricket, but men's cricket too, and also other sports. I've worked on lacrosse, netball, did some of the football World Cup and I want to do more on-screen stuff as I really like presenting."

It's a great sales pitch for freelance work, and, on the face of it, Georgie has it all. She's hugely talented, knowledgeable and she absolutely loves the work, but she knows that she has created obstacles for herself, and that these obstacles can grow bigger and wider. "I know there's something in my head that tells me I want to look thinner, but I also know that people won't hire me if I look too thin or too ill. People have told me this before. Someone told it to me very drunkenly once, and I got very upset because it's not something I want to hear."

"But there's also the health risk, isn't there? I mean, the damage you can do to your heart?" I ask, because this is my main concern. I'd want to be sure she's looking after herself. "Yes, people don't want to hire someone if they don't believe they'll be able to the job, so I have to really think about that bit too." Inevitably, Georgie's solution is not to eat more, but to exercise more. "I'm trying to get more into doing strength classes," she tells me. This is her way of dealing with her appearance and it's the fundamental point she has fought for. She does not want to eat more, she will look for more suitable alternatives. Georgie's 'food' is work and her 'work' is food. "I've always been a long-distance runner rather than a sprinter, so that's far more my size and shape than anything else. And then obviously I have cricket as a mental support."

Georgie also has a dog, and he's there, sitting on her lap as she talks to me. "I got him just after lockdown," she tells me, stroking his head, "because I had to go home and that was very stressful too. He's my support dog, and he gave me some kind of purpose when I had no job." Covid, for a workaholic like Georgie, must have been torture.

Fortunately, as I write this at the end of 2024, Georgie is over in Australia, fully employed in avoiding the 'winter blues' and finding work on the summer game across the globe. I notice on her social media page that she is currently commentating on her first Women's Big Bash game. She's going to go far, in all senses of the word. Georgie is a fighter and a talented one, and I wish her all the luck in the world, although luck isn't something she needs to rely on.

Fred Rumsey

WHEN YOU LOOK THROUGH the history books at the cricketing greats, it's understandably the feats on the pitch that capture your imagination. Frederick Edward Rumsey wouldn't be in many people's all-time world 11. But if you wanted an all-singing, all-dancing man of the cricketing world, then you need look no further. Fred delighted on the pitch with his accurate left-arm fast bowling, claiming 100 wickets in three of his six seasons for Somerset, and he played five times for his country. It is this, combined with the pioneering work he did behind the scenes, that makes him one of the greatest unsung heroes of the cricketing world. Fred was the main instigator of a players' union, which took shape as the PCA (Professional Cricketers' Association), and one of the prime movers of the fine art of fund-raising and of the marketing of cricket. Although cricket made Fred, he repaid the game tenfold.

I travel by train to Tewkesbury on a typically damp March afternoon and am met by Coleen, Fred's wife of 58 years. She's a slim, small-framed woman with lively eyes and a welcoming smile. She's doubling up as my chauffeur, and I'm grateful for her time and her friendly manner. "Fred doesn't get out much anymore," she tells me as she drives the short distance to their home. He is waiting, all bushy moustache and hooded eyes: a giant of a man who, at 88, looms over me as he shakes my hand. He may use a frame to walk with and have trouble with his ageing eyes but "I can talk for ever," he tells me.

We sit in their kitchen-diner, my coat barely off when Coleen brings me a very welcome cup of tea and an apple-Danish, as Fred and I occupy one end of their large dining-table. It's a table that Fred commands. He's a man who requires space. It's easy to imagine the lavish dinners that have been eaten in this room, with fine food and champagne, Fred holding court, regaling his fellow diners with yarns of yesteryear, sharing priceless tales of the cricketing characters of his era. Dotted around the room are quirky works of art or papier mâché dolls that take pride of place on the well-stacked shelves. They not only make it homely, but also are testament to a lifetime of family care and warmth. "My daughter is a very talented doll-maker," claims Fred proudly, as I examine some of the vast array of creations. It's such a down-to earth, wholesome scene that I'm lost for a while in domestic niceties. But Fred has plenty to say, and he says it with a well-documented clarity. "My grandfather was a 6-foot 6-inch heavyweight amateur boxing champion of London. He died before my father was married, and my dad took on looking after his six siblings when he was in his early twenties. He and his next-eldest brother were the only two earners, and they ran the family. His oldest sister became the 'mother'. He delayed his own marriage to my mother because of running the family. He had a sense of humour, but he was basically a serious man."

Fred himself was born on 4 December 1935 in Stepney in the East End of London. "It was a minute before midnight, and the Bow bells were ringing." He tells me this as though recalling the very moment. He can't claim that memory, even if he can claim to be a Cockney. His family only lived there for a year before his father, a stevedore, bought a comfortable house in Barking, and Fred spent his childhood happily in semi-rural Essex. As well as being an extremely hard worker, his father was a very keen cricketer who, Fred recalls, played the odd game for Essex Second XI in his youth. In Barking, he played for Holbrook Athletic Club, a nomadic team of which he was president. This brief spell, before his father was stationed abroad for the whole of the war, was enough of a grounding to allow Fred to develop his love of the game. "During that time, I had this feeling for cricket which had been instilled in my early life by my father's involvement. I can't remember a time when I didn't have a bat in my hand," he says. It's a familiar tale: the cricket bug is a hard one to shake off once it takes hold.

Fred talks for a while about his older sister, who was also influenced by his father's love of cricket. She scored for Essex Over-50s, and, for about 40 years, for London club Wanstead. His mother, he tells me, was a delightful woman, who never had a bad word to say about anyone. He pauses and looks reflectively at his huge hands. "I had a bad upbringing, because I thought everybody in the world was gorgeous, thanks to her." It's a fine quality, I interject, and one that, on reflection, I'm sure has helped to make him open-minded when dealing with others.

Fred went to Westbury, a local junior school, at the same time as Bobby Moore. "When I left, they predicted a future soccer career for me and a cricket one for him. He was a very talented all-rounder who bowled a bit of medium-pace." I admit to not knowing that

Bobby Moore played cricket, and we laugh about the notion of 'what if?' for a while, wondering if Bobby would have played cricket for England. Fred then explains that, because his father worked in shipping, he was sent on a scholarship to a trade school.

"In those days there was a Coopers' Company School, which, like Merchant Taylors', was a trade school. Coopers made barrels, but the school needed money to buy textbooks. They approached the local authority, who agreed to give it money if it signed an agreement to admit a certain number of local authority scholarship pupils. I was one of the pupils who'd got good grades. They were a rugby school, so as soon as I left Westbury, I never played soccer again." Being a natural ball player, Fred excelled at rugby, and ended up playing for North Midlands (later for Worcestershire and Herefordshire), but he gave up rugby for good at the age of twenty-three. His interest in cricket, however, was too deeply embedded to vanish.

After he left school, Fred played for Wanstead, opening the bowling with Barry Knight, who ended up playing for Essex and England. Whilst Fred was there, they asked him if he would like to play for the Essex Second XI. It was here, in the county game, that Fred's hatred of cricket's ridiculous snobbery really took root.

"In the scorecard of the first game I played in Second XI cricket, my name was printed Mr FE Rumsey, and below me was Savill L. When I queried it, I was told that he was a professional and that I was a gentleman, an amateur. I remember thinking, 'How bloody pompous can you get?'" This was highlighted by Fred Titmus who, when he played his first game for Middlesex, was an amateur, but turned professional the day after he was picked. On the Saturday, the announcer said. "There's one change to the scorecard. For Mr FJ Titmus, there is Titmus FJ.' "Cricket," says Fred, "doesn't do itself any favours sometimes. Certainly, the MCC didn't." This was a big factor in the motivation behind Fred's drive towards the unionisation of professional cricket.

I'm conscious, though, that, before we discuss the PCA, I need to hear more about his early life, so I steer the conversation to post-school and early employment. Fred tells me cheerfully that his success on the cricket field was echoed in his career. He landed a job in marketing, with a company called Fownes Gloves, one of the biggest glove firms in the country. Soon after he joined, the company was asked by the City of London to sell their building because the Council wanted to pull it down in order to reveal the Guildhall building that was hidden behind it. "They offered good money," Fred tells me. And because there was already a Fownes factory established in Worcester, they moved the base there. Fred was involved in the arrangements and, due to his apparent management ability, was offered a role in charge of a Yeovil branch that Fownes were soon to take over.

"At that time, I was advertising manager, sales manager and warehouse manager; and every time they gave me a new role, they gave me a new member of staff. And I was only twenty-two at the time." He shrugs at me. "I'd go in in the morning with my staff, and by 11 am I was finished. I had nothing to do because I'd given the jobs to everybody else." Fred explained that he decided to complain to the manager, asking not to give him any more staff so that he himself could be gainfully employed. In response, his manager asked if he still played cricket. He replied that he hadn't for a whole season, so he was told to go and do exactly that. "I said, 'But I have to work,' and he said, 'Well, come in, do your work, go off and play cricket.' So I did." We both marvel at this 'dream position.' Certainly an ideal scenario for any cricket-lover.

Fred was obviously no shirker, and Fownes Brothers were keen to keep him happy. He'd also evidently made an impression in the cricket world, despite his break from playing. "I knew Mike Jones, who was later to become President of Worcestershire," Fred goes on to explain. "He was on to me about playing cricket again, so I told him what my company had said, and asked him who I should play for. He said that the Second XI were struggling for bowlers. I gave it a go, and I enjoyed it, and they obviously liked me, because they offered me a contract." There's clearly nothing wrong with Fred's memory, because he remembered that, although he was earning £2,000 a year in the textile business, had his own staff and the offer of running the company in Yeovil, he accepted a two-year contract at £300 a year to play cricket for Worcestershire. Good with figures he might be, but not exactly out to become a millionaire.

We talk for a while about the huge difference in salary, as well as the leap into the unknown that he'd taken. County cricket was far from full-time employment in those days, and Fred had a successful career with Fownes mapped out ahead of him. It could have been a big mistake, as the professional cricket path didn't always run smoothly; but he had enough business nous to back himself, even when his decision appeared to have initially backfired. He admits that he did reasonably well, but not well enough. "I wouldn't say I threw my heart and soul into it. After two years, they sacked me." He wasn't quite sacked; in fact, Worcestershire suggested that he play in Second XI cricket at £5 a match so for a while he became a freelance cricketer. At the same time, he joined Kidderminster CC in the Birmingham League as their professional. It was here, during a net session, that Fred's cricket was changed for ever.

"Kidderminster had a former pro before me, called Roy Tattersall, who was a Lancashire off-spinner who'd played several times for England. He was watching me in the nets, and he said, 'You don't swing the ball, and I don't understand why not.' I said, 'I've never swung it.' He asked me how I held it, so I showed him, and he said 'Well, of course you won't swing it. You've got it right inside your hand. Hold it on the end.' I said, 'I can't do that. It would fall out.' He said, 'Of course it won't.' So he shone one side, and put the shiny side facing there, and the rough side facing there, and then made me hold it at the end of my hand.'"

Fred, using a make-believe ball as an example in those huge hands of his, shows me how the ball didn't fall out and tells me how he'd run up and bowl at the stumps as usual, and it swung so much that it would have hit leg-slip. The second time he tried aiming at second slip, and he knocked the stumps clean out. "Roy told me, 'Your action is perfect for swinging a ball. All you weren't doing was holding it properly.' Nobody had explained that to me in the years that I'd been in professional cricket. It took a slow right-arm bowler to tell a left-arm fast bowler how to swing the ball." This clearly wouldn't be the case today, we agree.

Tattersall's intervention in Fred's career was timely. In his autobiography, *Sense of Humour, Sense of Justice*, he talks about a dark mood that had invaded him after being dropped by Worcestershire. It's hard to see it in the no-nonsense man in front of me, but he had felt extremely low. Not so low as to do nothing, though, and this is where he is different from many who face setbacks. Instead of wallowing, he wrote. He wrote poetry and sent letters to all the counties "in the hope that one of them would take me on to their staff", he confesses in his book. The simple change in his grip turned out to be the pivotal moment.

Soon after, Worcestershire contacted Kidderminster, asking if they could pick Fred for a county match as they were in the race for the title and were short of an opening bowler. In that match, Fred took four wickets in the first innings and seven in the second and, unsurprisingly, the county side was keen to have him back. Fred laughs as he tells me, "So I laid the terms down, and said, 'I'll only come back if you guarantee me first-team cricket', but the committee wouldn't do it." Fred seems to have been resigned but not disappointed by this bureaucracy. Shortly after, he explains, Harold Stephenson, who was captain of Somerset, heard about what had happened and contacted him, agreeing to the same conditions Fred had suggested to Worcestershire, with the proviso that, if he was hopeless, he'd give them the option of dropping him. "Somerset offered me a three-year contract. And, in the first three months, I got 80 wickets. They kept me for six years. England picked me in my second year with Somerset. That's how things work." Fred raises his arms in mock despair, "I mean, you go from being fired to playing for England within two years, and it was all down to Roy Tattersall teaching me how to swing the ball."

"And so you moved to Taunton. When did you meet Coleen?" I ask as she enters the room. "In 1964," he says. I ask about when they got married and he replies, "It was 1966. I was going to South Africa to coach, and this is the exact conversation. She said, 'I suppose you expect me to be around when you come back?' And I said, 'What do you mean?' She said, 'Well, I don't know whether I will. It's six months.' So I said, 'What are you suggesting?' 'Well, if there was a better commitment, I might stay around,' she told me. I said, 'What sort of commitment?' and she said, 'Well, if we were going to get married.' So I said, 'Are you proposing?' and she said, 'Well, I suppose I am.' So I said, 'All right, you make the arrangements and I'll marry you the week I get back.'"

Coleen nods as I look at her for confirmation. "Well, I knew he wanted to marry me," she smiles as she leans over Fred, her arm lightly touching his shoulder. "And I'm thinking, oh, he's too manly, or a bit wishy-washy, so I'm going to have to do it. I'm going to say, 'OK, why don't we get married?' And he agreed."

"I have the evidence," Fred announces triumphantly "because, when she proposed to me, an article appeared in a women's magazine, with her telling the story." Then they both tell me it's their 58th wedding anniversary the following day, and when I ask if they're doing anything special, Coleen answers, "I don't know. I leave that to Fred." It's obvious that their relationship is a fine balance of respect and clear role-definition. In his autobiography, Fred writes that, of the people at their wedding, 'Most of those present, and others, predicted not much more than a year of happy union,' but these two headstrong characters had other ideas. Neither one was a push-over, both very much wearing the trousers.

We have a bit of a break during which Coleen refreshes our drinks, and Fred has a moment of reflection. It's an important bit of reflection, though. It says everything in a few sentences.

"One of the things that has interested me over the years is that there are 713 people who played for England in 147 years, and you always think of the millions who would have loved to have done it. I'm very proud of the fact that I did it. I ended up being picked six times but played only five times. I'd have been happy just to have had the chance to do it once. The most important was the Old Trafford Test, the first one I played. For the rest of my life, that I did that has had an enormous bearing on my life. Enormous."

"In what way?" I ask him. "In all the ways you could possibly imagine," he replies. "In the way that, in business, people want to talk to an England cricketer. I found that, when I was in property, and particularly when I wanted financial help, it was very easy to get into banks in London for a meeting. We'd spend three quarters of an hour talking cricket, and five minutes getting the deal done. In that sense, it was extremely important."

We pause over this a bit, because it is the essence of what it's all about for Fred. He is a businessman, an ideas man, a doer. He has used cricket, and that is the secret of his success. But this isn't a one-way train. He holds a return ticket. On his journey, Fred was responsible for giving so much to cricket. "It's had a bearing socially as well," he continues. "Do you think of yourself as a member of a club of some sort?" I put to him. "Yeah, it's an unofficial masonry," he replies. "And it would apply to rugby players in the same way. The only thing is that, with cricketers, it's a smaller one than with most other sports. It's made a huge difference to everything I've done since, and still does." Strange perhaps, but I hadn't considered the 'England' in England cricketers. I hadn't thought of it as some sort of peerage, a key to unlocking so many doors. Fred would have been successful in anything he did, I'd concluded, but the gravitas and the rarity of being an England cricketer is what gave him the edge.

Hold that thought, I tell myself, and I ask him about his time with Somerset. He confirms that he was there for six years, and, despite him taking a total of 547 wickets at an average of just over 20, and reaching the 100-wicket mark in three seasons, the club went without silverware. It was in 1967, when Somerset lost to Kent in the Gillette Cup final, that Fred began to put into cricket some of what he'd taken out. "What happened was that we got into the final, but Somerset didn't have enough money to pay us any more for getting there. So I said to them, 'Would you give me the opportunity of raising more money for the players?'"

Fred has a glint in his eye. This is something he's very proud of, something he does well. "So the club asked, 'What have you got in mind?' and I said, 'Making a brochure that is solely funded by advertising, and selling it.' 'Oh, you couldn't make that work. Nobody's interested in being part of that.' So, I said, 'Well, could you give me a chance?' and they agreed. I sold all the advertising in about two hours."

I can almost imagine the calls, I tell him, and I ask how he managed it. "I just phoned people up and asked for the director responsible for advertising. I told them we were going up to Lord's and we were wanting to publish a brochure – and we'd like them to advertise in it. Not one of them turned me down. Not one. There was an enormous amount of support through industry and business, and nobody in cricket was tapping into it." It's hard to believe this, with the prevalence of sponsorship and advertising in cricket today; but there was an obvious gap, a money-spinner, and Fred, with such a good head for marketing, had spotted it. This was partly due to his training, but also to his powers of persuasion. Cricket was waking up to the importance of sponsorship, and Fred was ahead of the game.

"During the winter of 1967, I wrote a piece for Somerset on the possibilities of employing a public relations fundraiser, and then I applied for the job – and got it. I said to them, 'You don't have to find extra money to pay me. It will come out of the money I'll raise. The extra will go to the club.' They agreed, so I did it." "Did that make you more money than playing cricket?" I ask him, already sure of the answer. "Oh yeah, lots more, so, after that year went so well,

I asked if we could make it a permanent position. It went to the Committee, and I didn't hear back."

It was during this time that Fred's greatest contribution to cricket occurred. Perhaps geed by his success with the PR work, and being a man who wasn't scared to stand up for himself, he began the formation of the Professional Cricketers' Association. "As you know, I wasn't happy about the MCC. I knew that they ran first-class cricket and even though all the players were now professional, the administration remained amateur. I didn't feel that we had enough experience to run our game. The amateur administrators were, for the most part, people who loved cricket. Just occasionally, you came across a good businessman, but you needed a good half-dozen." He was thinking about this, he explains, when the players were having trouble with their food at Somerset. "We had to share our lunches with spiders and flies. Anything that crawled got onto our plates, and we were eating translucent potatoes, boiled so long they had no goodness left in them. We'd had enough, so we went on strike and sent the twelfth man down to the fish-and-chipper to get our lunch. The club weren't very happy about that," smiles Fred. He was nominated by the players to discuss it with the Secretary. He told him that they refused to eat the rubbish produced, suggesting that they employ a caterer, and when the Secretary said it was a matter of cost, Fred suggested getting the meals sponsored.

This battle, which he won, made him think about the game as a whole, how there was no one who stood up to anyone, nor anyone who had a say in the players' future. He decided to set about forming a union. To do this, he wrote to each county, addressing one letter to the Secretary (equivalent to today's CEO) and one to the senior pro. Fred explained that he painstakingly followed up these letters in person. "When I played against each county, I asked if I could have a meeting with the team during our visit. Over the 1966 season, I put my case face-to-face. I did the same the following year, to any counties I'd missed during the 1967 season." At the end of these negotiations, Fred organised a big meeting in Fleet Street, managing to talk the *Daily Express* into covering the various costs by offering them an exclusive article. He persuaded Jimmy Hill (chair of the Professional Footballers' Association) and Cliff Lloyd (secretary of the PFA) to come along and talk to everyone following the meeting, which was chaired by Sussex's wicket-keeper-batter Jim Parks.

The PCA was formed, and Fred became General Secretary. Roger Prideaux was elected chair, and Jack Bannister became treasurer.

It wasn't long before the PCA was making an impact. The first discussion Fred had with the MCC was over the Sunday League, which came in almost immediately the union was formed. Fred remembers that, at the time, Somerset were playing Kent. "I had to come off the field three times to negotiate. I told Billy Griffith, who was the MCC Secretary, that I wanted a minimum of £400 extra for my members if they were to play in this new competition. It meant, after all, that there would be no day off, and they'd be getting no financial reward. The MCC reckoned £200 was enough, but they finally agreed to £400. That was the first time the players had taken on, collectively, the administration, and won their case." The magnitude of this victory isn't lost on me. Fred had worked hard to make this happen, and I can't pretend I don't feel an overwhelming sense of admiration for this hard-working man, this Robin Hood.

"Was part of the remit to include provision for players post-cricket?" I ask. "I had that in mind as well," he replies. "It was part of my brief that it would continue when players had retired or if they were forced out of the game by injury. That was a big issue, one that worried me a lot. Insurance, and the fact that players could lose revenue by being injured." "Like your friend, Colin Milburn, losing his eye?" I suggest. "Not just that, I was thinking of pulled muscles that weren't treated properly at the time." Another thing Fred was keen to highlight was the disparity between counties: Warwickshire had doctors and physiotherapists, Somerset had only a dressing-room attendant. Fred tells me he was concerned that some players were missing out on vital care.

He worked tirelessly for the PCA for a year but, after Somerset spent so long dragging their heels over renewing his marketing role for the second year, he replied to Derbyshire's advertisement for a PR fundraiser. The club was to celebrate its centenary in 1970 and needed help to organise events. After three interviews, and seeing off 1,000 applicants, Fred got the job. "I was an ex-international by that time, I understood the game, and I'd done the job at Somerset the winter before, plus I was still able to play." It was a no-brainer, he explains. When he accepted the job, he was immediately put on the employment side. Fred, being a principled man, didn't feel that it was right that he should be both an employer and, at the same time, the representative of the union. He withdrew. "I didn't hear anything from the PCA for years. I remember they thanked me for forming it and asked if I would accept honorary life-membership. I said yes, very nice of you. It was twenty years later that Coleen suggested to the then-CEO, that it might be a good idea to make me an Honorary Vice-President."

When he left Somerset, Fred played one three-day match for Derbyshire, then featured regularly in the Sunday League and the one-day knockout competitions, alongside his fundraising and PR position. He continued in that role for five years before deciding to work in property. First, he found someone to replace him, then withdrew totally. "But not entirely from cricket?" I ask. "Apart from the Lord's Taverners," he answers. "That was the charity I worked for, and my three forms of revenue became property, travel and PR."

Keen to stick to cricket, I ask if the travel involved going to cricket grounds. "The travel was going all over the world, but not necessarily to cricket grounds," he replies. "We ran England cricket travel for a while, for the players and the press." "It's interesting," I add, "how many ex-cricketers go into travel. Perhaps it's to do with the number of places you've seen, or the many contacts you made." As if to illustrate this, he tells me about the Cricket Festival he started in Barbados. It was called the Fred Rumsey Pro Cricket Festival, and it ran for thirty-two years. "It only happened as a result of the Lord's Taverners' activities. We were involved in raising money for buses for disabled children by sponsoring races. We went to Oulton Park race track, where the manager, Rex Foster, introduced me to his son, who ran a travel company. He was keen to get some cricketers to go to Barbados, and he outlined the sort of festival he wanted. I suggested he needed a flagship event to sell to the cricket clubs, and I offered to do the PR if he did the travel. He said it would be wonderful if I did. This was on a Tuesday. By Friday, the pair of us were in Barbados, speaking to the cricket authorities there. Peter Short was a very famous West Indian cricket administrator, and I told him what we wanted to do. He warned us that festival cricket didn't work well in Barbados and he only gave it a couple of years. I reminded him of that conversation after our first ten years, and I reminded him again at the end of twenty-one years, and again after thirty!" It developed into a really impressive festival, with many of the great players and a plethora of stars of screen and stage involved. Fred shows me the photos and the newspaper clips. It's an amazing legacy, and those hooded eyes sparkle with a multitude of memories.

Through his connections over the years, Fred set up in Barbados a company which he called Sport Barbados. He was contacted by John Taylor, who was a Lord's Taverner, asking him to talk to Shell Barbados, who had recently lost the sponsorship of the cricket and felt they had also lost their identity. Taylor asked him if he'd advise them on what to do. Fred told me that he wrote them three proposals. One was to get involved with tourism. The second was to get involved with art, particularly young people's art. The third was to set up a football tournament. They went for the football tournament and asked him to organise it. "So I wrote the rules and we formed a thing called the Shell Caribbean Cup, which ran from 1989 to 1994." I ask whether he thought it a success, and he explains that it was a sell-out, and that "Shell rode the moon." It's a lovely phrase, I tell him. I can almost see it lit up on a hoarding.

Fred knows how to sell. It's not just the amount he seems to do, it's the scale that blows my mind. "Do you think you have a bit of a reputation as someone who takes on things?" I laugh, and then I follow up with, "You didn't skimp on the work, did you? You did a bit of everything." This makes him think for a moment, reaching back into the distant past. "Well, I was trained to sell. Someone told me once that the more stones you turn over on a beach, the more crabs you find. That stuck in my mind. I started my own business when I left Fownes in my early twenties and joined Worcestershire. I bought a shop in Worcester, cleaning and fitting carpets, which I ran when I wasn't playing cricket."

I tell him that, for most people, owning a business at the same time as playing cricket is quite enough to be going on with, but Fred's work ethic isn't average. "When I started working for myself, I thought – well, if I don't get up in the morning, I don't make any money." I question him here, because I knew it wasn't necessarily the money that he worked so hard for, and he agrees. "No, I'm not interested in money. But you need it to run a family. When we were married with three kids, I bought a very nice house with about eight acres. I worked on the land and sold the produce, and I used to get up at six o'clock in the morning, plus I had a full-time gardener, and he and I would work until about half past eight. Then I'd have a shower. I'd possibly have a bit of breakfast, then go to work and come home."

For some people, cricket is the start, the middle and the end. It shapes their lives, and it makes them who they are. This isn't the case with Fred. A single focus was never going to be enough in that busy head of his, but it was a big part of his life. It was an enabler, and it gave him the kudos to be successful in everything he went on to do. "You've had an incredibly full life," I tell him. "Well, I've had an enjoyable one."

The special feeling, that moment in time that stays with you for ever, that is what defines us, and Fred makes such a moving tribute to cricket that it makes the hair on the back of my neck stand up. "Outside of the normal things, like marriage and the birth of your children, and of their children, the most important thing was walking out in my first Test at Old Trafford. When I closed the gates behind me, I remember thinking, 'No one can take the three lions away'. In a sense, that completed my ambition." He is so wistful as he says this that I can almost picture the turf under his feet as he made his way out to the middle, his heart racing. He could have given up cricket then and there, he tells me. But he didn't, fortunately for cricket.

Before I leave, he shows me a bulging scrapbook of his cricketing career, full of articles lovingly collected by his sister. A Rumsey archive. "I'm doing this with my grandson," he tells me, as he turns over page after page of yellowing headlines. "We've been through it and created it, and now it's going to be put into book form." It's big, as you can imagine, and, within its pages, it documents the life of a man who held cricket to account. He looked to unravel the tangles of a class-led cricket world, where professional cricketers were run by amateur bosses. And he helped to give those cricketers the armour they needed to thrive in the game. At the same time, he helped to inject essential cash into a poorly funded domestic system, through sponsorship and publicity. And yes, cricket might have made him great, but there's no doubt he deserved it. He's a giant of a man.

Sue Redfern

I REMEMBER ONCE drawing an illustration of a cricket match in progress. As well as the opening batters, I had eleven players strategically placed in the field: mid-on, mid-off, mid-wicket, a bowler in full stride, the batter reaching forward, a rather oversized bat defending the wicket, with the keeper up to the stumps. Cover-point was there, gully and two slips with a questionable gap between them, and a couple of boundary riders in front of the crowd that I'd painstakingly included, some standing, some sitting. It was a somewhat crude attempt at a stylised descriptive cartoon. Only later did I realise that I'd made an error. I hadn't included the umpires. That got me thinking. Umpires are a bit like wicket-keepers. If they do their job efficiently, they are easily overlooked. In reality, though, umpires are essential to the sport. True, there's rarely a game of cricket in which all the umpiring decisions are unquestionably right, but cricket still needs umpires.

Given the controversies that inevitably surround umpires, what makes someone want to be one? I've always shied away from conflict, so it's something I've never understood. In friendly cricket the onus of umpiring usually falls on members of the team. Some take it on willingly. There are contrasting views in my own family: my son is keen to umpire (it keeps him involved in the game if he's been out cheaply), whereas my husband shirks from what he sees as a task too far. His preference is to sit back and enjoy the game, leaving the tough decisions to those who relish the challenge and risk the backlash.

What could be more perilous than the role of a female umpire in the men's game? It requires a special sort of person to take that plunge. You're not just an umpire making a 'bad decision'. You're making a bad decision because you're a woman.

Sue Redfern is apparently impossible to pin down. It seems that every time I am available to meet, she is involved in a match in another part of the country or in another country entirely. This is because, as the only full-time female umpire employed by the ECB, she is in demand in the women's game and now in the men's as well. In September 2023, she became the first female umpire to stand in a first-class game in England and Wales. The groundbreaking occasion was a match between Glamorgan and Derbyshire at Sophia Gardens,

Cardiff. Sue had jumped over the wall and landed on her feet on the sacrosanct turf of men's cricket. It's an impressive achievement, one which brings with it the prospect that other women will follow in her capable footsteps.

After meeting very briefly at the Women's ODI at Taunton in May, where Sue was umpiring, we finally settle for a Zoom conversation in December, with Sue in a hotel in Sylhet, the evening before a Women's T20I between Bangladesh and Ireland, and me, fresh from breakfast, in England. The hotel Wi-Fi is a challenge; Sue is a delight.

Sue Redfern was born in Mansfield in October 1977, but spent her childhood in Kimberley, a few miles from Nottingham. She was one of two children, her brother Mike the elder by two years. Her family was "very much working class", she tells me, her mum a hairdresser who owned her own hair salon, her dad a car mechanic who was in haulage logistics. "Both my parents were pretty sporty," she explains, "and it would be fair to say every single penny they earned was spent on Mike and me playing a lot of sport. They encouraged us to take up whatever we wanted, although I wasn't allowed to play rugby because my mum was concerned about injury. My dad was an umpire when I was growing up, but he also used to play to a high level. He managed to get as far as the Nottinghamshire Second XI. But my mum wasn't really interested in cricket, and I'd say my brother was probably more into cricket than I was. But by the time I got to sixteen, cricket was my main choice."

And choices she definitely had. She's not wrong about being sporty. As a child growing up, her two main sports were swimming and badminton. She excelled at both, so much so that she had a decision to make about her future at the same time as taking her GCSEs. "At sixteen I was offered a scholarship to go to play badminton at a university in America, and I made the choice not to go. At that point cricket had really taken over, because I started playing for England at a young age." A 'sliding doors' moment then. I always like these. I'm fascinated by the 'what ifs' of life. I'd imagine that most people would jump at the chance of studying a sport they enjoyed in a foreign country. But there were circumstances that Sue later revealed which probably guided her decision-making.

For a while I ask her about how hard she found it to prioritise one particular sport when she obviously excelled in a few, but it's clear that cricket had started to get under her skin by then. "How did you get into cricket? Was that through your dad?" I ask, assuming that he was her driving force. But Sue thinks her brother's influence was probably stronger. "It was more to do with my brother and choosing the sport that he was playing. We played at the same club, first at Kimberley and then at Eastwood Town, in different teams. And like I say, whatever sport we chose to have a go at, Mum and Dad would always support us."

I understand this. Much of my childhood was spent in the garden or up the road with my brother, and there was the same age difference between us as between Sue and Mike. My brother was my playmate as a kid, so what he liked, I liked too. Sue and her brother were very dedicated, and her parents were willing to facilitate that dedication. "There'd be days when my brother would be playing in one team for the cricket club, and I'd be playing in another. Mum would go with my brother, and Dad would come with me, and they would cross each other on the motorway to switch at half time. It was kind of chaotic really." Chaotic maybe, but it's a great image.

The pressure of time and the multiple car scenes remind me of the film *Clockwise*, with Sue's dad played by an exasperated and exasperating John Cleese and her mum by a long-suffering Penelope Wilton. It's a scenario that has been acted out with variations across the whole of society, parents sacrificing their time to enable their children to participate in their desired sport. "So, your parents were really key to your sporting development," I say, as a statement rather than a question. "Yes, pivotal. And I suppose it's still the same today for young people to have that parental support. It's not just that they provide the transport, it's the flexibility that is so important in allowing children to have access to their sport." She knows how unlikely it is that that she would have progressed without them.

Sue went to the local junior school, so her experience of cricket during her state education was typically limited, but she tells me a story that gave her some insight into the trials of men's cricket. "My first experience of cricket was playing Kwik Cricket on astroturf. We were lucky. The teacher, Sam Jamieson, was a family friend, and he loved cricket. I remember I came on to bowl, and it was typical if I played in boys' cricket for the opposition to laugh at a girl bowling, which helped me really because I surprised them by getting wickets. But this one time, I bowled a ball and hit the batter between the legs, and he went down like a lead balloon. The teacher of the other school came across and thanked me, saying, 'I've been trying to get him to wear a box for quite some time, but you've made things a whole lot easier.' So that was my junior school experience. And yes, we played a little bit, but nothing serious. My playing took off at club level."

Although Sue's dad had played cricket to a good standard, she doesn't remember him playing. But she does remember him umpiring in league matches. "As a child, if Mum needed a baby-sitter, then Dad had to bring me to the cricket while he was umpiring. I remember he plonked me on the side of the outfield, gave me some pocket money and told me not to leave the ground. That was his only instruction in those days." This makes me laugh as it matches my own childhood in some respects (although I usually had the rest of my family around). As soon as my dad was on the cricket field, that was him gone for the day, I could be hanging upside down from the pavilion and he wouldn't have noticed. But those early days, when the outdoors captures your imagination and the warm days slide into long shadows, there's something so captivating about a game going on in front of you, its intricacies and dramas invading your own games in a comforting parallel universe.

When I ask Sue if it was something she enjoyed, her answer echoes mine. "It was time with my dad. You know, you make your own fun as a child, don't you? I'd get to sit on the roller with the groundsman doing the rolling and I got to experience different things, you learn what it is to be part of a club." If I nod any harder my head may topple, I think. I'd go further. I'd say these are the essential times, when the game enters your being so completely that you won't ever lose it. My mind goes off on tangents of subconscious childhood influence. I find myself wondering where and when the spark of interest first glowed. Although we don't discuss this, I can't help thinking it's no coincidence that Sue will go on to be one of the most well-known female umpires in history. The umpiring gene was clearly implanted early.

It feels important that Sue had that early exposure to cricket, a kind of armour for when she began playing her youth cricket in the late 1980s and early 1990s. Although it is nearly a decade later than my own experience of playing men's cricket, it would still have been a rare occurrence for a girl to be involved in club cricket. Prior knowledge of the game seems likely to have put her on a more level playing field. "Was it tough, or were they welcoming?" I ask. "They were brilliant," she replies unequivocally. I played under-13s, under-15s and under-18s boys' cricket, mostly in the Second XI. My brother played in the First XI. I was also the First XI scorer, when available, so I'd get some pocket money and watch my brother play. But yeah, they were brilliant. Mike and I rarely played in the same team, but we did play in the under-18s together, and I have fond memories of that time. One particular memory was when we played in the league's cup final against a rival team called Heanor Town. I was a bowler and wasn't expected to bat. My brother was the opening batter. We were batting second and needed a few runs to win, but we kept losing wickets, so I ended up batting with my brother. I remember, in a typical older brother way, he walked up to me and said, 'Whatever you do, don't get out', and I was, 'OK. Thanks for that piece of advice.' I had eighteen-year-old boys bowling bouncers at my head, and I'm fifteen at the time. There were no helmets in those days and I'm petrified because I wasn't a batter then, and you know I'm almost in tears and my brother's walking down the wicket telling me not to get out." Her team won, Sue informs me. Quite a result.

I have long been an advocate of mixed cricket. I think it provides essential experience both for the game and for life; experience that helps to make cricket a sport for all. Even so, it remains clear that if you are genuinely talented and wish to excel, single-gender cricket is still the best option. I ask Sue if she had played for a women's team as well. "No," she answers, "I started playing boys' cricket probably at age eleven and played that exclusively until I was about thirteen. There weren't any local girls' teams around then. It was when we moved to Derbyshire and I'd been playing in club leagues in the summer that my mum and dad sat me down and said, 'We've found this newspaper article, and it says that there's a women's cricket club setting up in Derby. Would you be interested in women's cricket?' So I went to the net sessions in the winter and joined Derby Women's Cricket Club." She went on to play for them for sixteen years. But, as she explains, it was quite a change to begin with. With so few young girls playing cricket, she found that there was a ridiculously big age gap. "I was thirteen, and the next age group to me was around twenty-five. Women's cricket has changed so much now, with so many more players in their teens, but at the time it was effectively me playing with adults."

Sue knew the game well enough to be confident in her ability, and she thrived in the environment she found herself in. She says that her performance on the field was greatly enhanced by playing cricket in an adult team. "You know, obviously they're formative years, aren't they? From the age of thirteen, I was on a cricket field all day with these adults, and they were incredible with me." Sue got the support she needed to progress to a higher level with a dedicated team and coach. "This Derby women's team stayed together for about fifteen years, and it was just such good fun. When I look back at the choice I was given between playing badminton in America or staying with this cricket team, I have no regrets. Badminton is a very individual sport, and for me team sport was what I enjoyed. It's just bigger than the actual playing, if that makes sense." I can't argue with this. I too am a great believer in the human value of team sports.

I was keen to find out how different Sue felt it was playing for a women's team rather than the boys' team, and she is completely honest and quick with her answer. "Well, in those days it wasn't comparable really. Boys' cricket was faster, and the ball was hit harder." She was clear that this did not detract from the technical skill involved in women's cricket.

"The level of the cricket I played at Derby and then for the East Midlands Women was pretty good. We had an impressive nucleus of players and, along with Yorkshire, Nottingham, Surrey and Thames Valley, there were some really strong women's county teams. It's as difficult to compare men's and women's cricket as it is to compare generations. I look now at the modern game, and I know that there are players of my generation who would absolutely slot into women's cricket today, but not without some obvious changes. The fitness has improved so much. The athleticism and the dynamics of the game are unrecognisable. When I first started, we were playing 60-over cricket and 200 was a good score. The expectation, the strike rates and what you could do with cricket, was totally different." There's no doubt that that's true. The sense of freedom in cricket has greatly expanded, partly as a result of the England men's Bazball approach, but also because the physicality, the equipment and the egos have changed. With the essential finances and the appropriate focus now being given to them, women have become far more adept at all levels of the game. "When I was playing, our generation followed tradition. If you wanted to be creative with your shot-making it was frowned upon," Sue admits. Frowned is a good word. Cricket does a lot of frowning.

It's often the case, as it was with the Derby women's team, that the formation of a cricket team relies upon the dedication and expertise of one person. At Derby that person was Sue Witham, who coached Sue throughout her time at Derby and then when that club took on the county mantle of Derbyshire. Sue is full of praise for her coach: "She was instrumental in me having the opportunities I had in women's cricket."

With Sue Witham's encouragement, Sue made her County Championship debut for East Midlands when she was only thirteen and new to the women's game.

Championship Cricket for women was wholly different from the long-established men's version. "In the women's game, County Championship fixtures were run over one week, so you'd play five days of cricket in one week and that was your County Championship season over with. There were twelve grounds used for twenty-four teams over the course of that time. I played for East Midlands, although in the first year I was just twelfth. But by the time I got into the second year, I was opening the bowling with Jo Chamberlain, who at the time was England's opening bowler. And I was playing with Karen Smithies, who was the England women's captain, Jane Smit, the England wicket-keeper, and there were also great characters of the game like Wendy Watson and Enid Bakewell." A few years into Sue's playing for East Midlands, more county teams were formed, gradually augmenting the County Championship. When Derbyshire was formed in 1997, Sue left East Midlands to join them.

It was without much trouble that Sue had made it into the county scene. "How did you break into the England side?" I ask, wondering if it had been harder graft. "It was all pretty surreal, to be honest," she laughs. "At the end of the County Championship week, where all the counties had played together in clubs across Cambridge, we all came together on the evening of the last game, when the awards got handed out for the winners and for the players of the tournament. We were sitting out on the grass and then they named the England squad there and then, because the tours are straight after the Championship finishes. I was sitting on the grass, and my name was called out for an England selection."

Sue admits that she was shocked to be selected at the age of sixteen, and we both discuss how random and somehow haphazard it seems. "Afterwards," she explains, "you get put into a changing-room and you're told what's going to happen, what you need to do and how much you will need to pay." Selection, it seems, was largely based on your performance during the Championship week. Sue went on to play a bit of what she calls junior England, "which meant a training week of cricket where you were given bibs to wear with numbers on, and during the week numbers were called and there would be fewer and fewer of us, until the ones left are the squad." There appears to have been a lot of name- and number-calling, and it sounds pretty brutal. The awful feeling as a kid when you're bibbed-up ready to play in a team, only to be overlooked as those around you are touched on the head. I remember that in netball. This was England-level though, not playground pursuits. Fortunately, it's a world away from how it is now.

It's clear that Sue was fairly overwhelmed by being chosen as part of the England squad. Not wanting to belittle this achievement, I suggest that being a woman cricketer in the twentieth century wasn't straightforward, or at least didn't feel like a significant step on your career path. It was an expense you paid because it was doing something you loved. "How did you afford it?" I ask, aware of Sue's background. "It was expensive, but not the same as the generation before me. I had to pay for a blazer and a little bit of travel. I didn't have to pay for full tours." Once again, Sue pays homage to the support from her parents. But it was just at this exciting time that she had to make some serious decisions. A change in her family circumstances meant that she had to repay that debt rather sooner than she had expected.

Sue was just sixteen when she first played for England: the age at which she was offered the badminton scholarship at an American university and also the age at which she was due to take her GCSEs. But this was when her dad, in his early fifties, fell ill. "I had just started to do my A levels, but because my dad could no longer work, I came out of school and took a casual job." With her dad incapacitated, Sue needed to earn an income in order to continue to play cricket without being a burden on her parents. "Was he poorly for long?" I ask. "Oh yeah, he didn't work again," she explains. "It was a difficult time. My brother had got a scholarship to Repton to play cricket, so financially it was tough, but also supporting someone who was ill was difficult." She doesn't dramatise this, and she doesn't offer further details and so I respect Sue's and the family's privacy. This isn't about Sue; there's no 'poor me', no sense that she is telling me this to gain sympathy. It happened, and this was how she dealt with it. The fact that it created an upheaval in her so-far-comfortable upbringing is unsaid. Sue went on to get three part-time jobs so that she could be flexible to play cricket. "What were your three jobs?" I ask, wondering whether they involved sport. "I had a couple of lifeguard sports-centre jobs, and I also worked as a cricket coach for Derbyshire schools, a kind of early Chance to Shine without the logo."

She first played for England in a 1995 European Championship Tournament in Ireland, where she picked up an injury. Luckily, she recovered in time to be selected to make her Test debut against India in 1995. At the age of 17 she embarked on a seven-week tour of India with a group of women whom, only a year before, she had watched as her heroes. "It was an incredible experience," Sue says, "to be there with such icons of the game, but luckily I'd known a number of them since I'd started playing for Derby, so I wasn't too overwhelmed."

Sue played a total of six Test matches and fifteen ODIs. Her best performance was during an ODI series against South Africa in 1997, when she took 9 wickets at an average of just 10.44, including a best of 4 for 21 from 10 overs. She also took part in four of the seven games of the Women's World Cup in India at the end of 1997. She was only twenty-one when she played her final match for England in 1999. "It's quite an age to retire," I remark, conscious that it would be the usual age for the start of an international career, and when I ask her why she stopped playing so young, everhonest Sue replies, "It was basically fitness and deselection. I've never been the slimmest of individuals, and I think England wanted to go in a different direction. Plus, I had a couple of niggles, and I was just a Joe average medium pacer."

The year 2000 may have heralded a new millennium, but not a whole lot had changed in the women's game when Sue found herself out of the England side. She went back to playing for her county, but she was aware that the career opportunities for women in the sport were few and far between. The need to be financially self-sufficient saw her seeking other avenues, and she joined the civil service. It was a few years later, when she was playing for one of her clubs, that she met Helen Pack who was working for the ECB (now, one of only two female ECB match referees) and Sue was able to reconnect and follow what sounds like a dream job.

She began working for the ECB in 2005 as their regional women's and girls' manager. Then the role morphed: "I became national lead for women's and girls' development alongside Clare Connor. We split the women's cricket development and the performance teams. I took over the development. Clare was in control of the performance. Then in 2013, I moved to an inclusion role." Sue had been given an important position in the inner sanctum, just as the ECB was increasing its work force significantly. Along with Connor, she was involved in planting the seeds of change in the women's game, "I was able to support women's and girls' cricket and help to grow it as much as possible." This would have been a fascinating and rewarding time to be involved in the administration of the game, but, having finished playing all forms of cricket, she was missing the experience on the pitch.

Sue had finished playing for Derbyshire in 2005 after an injury that put her out for a year. She moved to Staffordshire and then snapped an Achilles tendon playing badminton. After fourteen weeks in a cast, she hobbled away from county cricket but continued with club cricket for a few years longer. She came to the end of her playing days by the age of thirty-five, but as she explains, "I still wanted to stay involved in the game. I initially finished playing in 2010, had a season off, missed it, then came back in 2012. But in the end it just wasn't worth the pain of playing. So, over the winter of 2012, knowing I still wanted to stay involved, but not as a scorer or as a coach, I picked up the phone to Dad and told him I was thinking of umpiring. I asked him what he thought, and he said, 'Just give it a go and see what you think.' And so, in the winter of 2012, I took my qualification with Warwickshire, my local county association. And then, in May 2013, I made my on-field debut as an umpire in the local league, and it was one of the scariest things I'd ever done in my life."

I can readily imagine the sense of responsibility that goes along with umpiring, but to turn up as a woman must have been doubly hard. Sue paints the picture well. "I joined the Warwickshire

Cricket League panel of umpires, and they appointed me to Aston University CC playing at home. I turned up and got mistaken for the scorer! They couldn't believe I was the umpire. I met my colleague there for the first time, and we went out and did the pitch inspection." It's the preconceived ideas that are so hard to challenge. I myself have been thanked for the tea at games when I've had nothing to do with it. I've been told the laws and asked which player I was dating time and time again, but I've not had the power to affect the game, to make a real impact. That has to be scary, especially when most people are expecting you to fail. It's not that people want you to, or that they are cruel, but if you're a trailblazer then you are challenging the norm, and there's a load of 'norm' involved in sport.

People aren't used to seeing female officials. It's tough to be the first one, and that's why it's so impressive. Sue didn't go on to bathe herself in glory during the game, but the relatively low quality of the cricket probably went some way to calming her nerves. "I had no idea what I was doing to be perfectly honest. I was quite surprised how many different laws existed. But I took the bowler's end, and I was waiting for him to start bowling and then my colleague shouted over from square leg, 'You've got to call play.' I had no idea what standard the cricket was going to be because I hadn't been involved for years in men's cricket, and without a word of a lie, the first bowler comes running in off a very long run and it was the slowest delivery I've ever seen in my life. The batter jumped out the way and was bowled! I couldn't believe the level of cricket; I mean it started at 12.30 and I was home at 3 o'clock."

After a year in the Warwickshire League, Sue moved to the league above, which was the Birmingham District Premier League. "And how were you received generally?" I ask. "Mostly really well. I've always found one of the benefits of being female in men's cricket is the behaviour changes. They behave a little better. They apologise when they swear, which I find quite funny because I swear a lot. It's hard to know whether it was because I was female or new, but I used to get more appeals. If you go to a new environment, you tend to get tested more often. One of the captains said to me that they don't bother to appeal too often at me because they can't influence me. I took that as a real compliment, because that's how it should be in my opinion."

It was in this first year, though, that Sue was severely tested when she was physically abused by an irate player. "I gave an lbw, which I didn't think was at all controversial," she begins. "He walked off moaning, and his colleague, who was at the non-striker's end, looked at me and said, 'I don't know what he's moaning about, it was plumb.' I thought it was a really innocuous straightforward decision. At the end of the game as we were shaking hands, the aggrieved player grabbed my arm and wouldn't let it go. He gave me a torrent of verbal abuse, telling me what he thought of me." Sue was really shaken, and even more upset when her colleague didn't back her up. "The league was great though," she tells me. "I rang them and explained what had happened, and they said, 'Regardless of your colleague not supporting you, we're going to follow through with this, as it's unacceptable.' And within twenty-four hours, the league had written to the club. The club agreed it had happened, and the player was banned for the rest of the season."

Officials should never be made to feel vulnerable. Thankfully the league handled the situation well, but Sue was not far from stepping down. "I'd been given a mentor by Warwickshire Umpires, and without his intervention and support I don't think I'd have carried on."

Sue continued to umpire in the Birmingham League, gaining confidence with experience, even being chosen to be fourth official in some international matches. She was also put onto the national panel which included some Second XI men's cricket. She was yet to break into women's international cricket however, and when the invitation came it was out of the blue. "I was working from home one day, and I got an e-mail from somebody at the ICC. They said, 'Congratulations, you've been invited to the Women's World Cup qualifiers in Thailand.' I rang the National Umpires Manager at the ECB, who'd obviously given them my details, but even he didn't know I'd been appointed. It's all changed nowadays. It's a very different process, but that was how I started."

It wasn't long before she was umpiring at the very pinnacle of the women's game. In January 2017, she umpired in the Women's World Cup, some twenty years after she had played in it. Sue admits she felt very privileged to be at the heart of the tournament, especially since it was in England. She went from strength to strength in women's international cricket, being included as part of the umpiring team at the Women's World T20 Cup and officiating at the first-ever game of The Hundred in July 2021.

In 2022, she was offered a full-time umpiring role by the ECB. That was when, as she tells me, "I left my day job." She is still the only woman to have this position. There has been much talk about the different pay-scales in the men's and women's games, and Sue makes some interesting points when I ask her about this. "The ICC are recognising how quickly women's cricket is growing, especially the commercial side, so they are looking to move toward pay parity. Men's cricket is slightly different in terms of skill-sets but the women's game is still an elite sport." I've never understood why one person can be paid more than another for doing the same job. And Sue agrees. "The roles I have are exactly the same in the men's game as they are in the women's." Although she is confident that the ICC is looking for parity, it must be odd for her to receive so much more in one form of the game than in the other.

In 2023 Sue crossed that great divide and was the first female umpire to stand in a first-class game when she officiated Glamorgan v Derbyshire at Sophia Gardens. There are several firsts in Sue's CV, all of them impactful, but somehow this one feels the biggest. I ask Sue how she felt about that step. "It's great because it demonstrates that there are genuine opportunities regardless of gender in the game. Although the skills needed for men's or women's cricket are different, if you're good enough then you can demonstrate that as an official you don't have to be a certain gender."

As someone who is always looking to improve, Sue's a fan of the Decision Review System (DRS) in cricket, seeing it as a chance to look at the mistakes that you've made in games. "Umpires are humans, they aren't always right. DRS helps to identify errors and look at patterns and certain scenarios. I work hard to improve, and the technology helps with this. To be honest, I'm really lucky to have it available to me."

When we come to the end of our chat, I feel I have learnt a lot about Sue. She quietly embodies the changing face of women's cricket. Her years in the game cover the era that has witnessed the growing movement towards gender equality, and Sue has helped to shape that movement by being brave enough (and believe you me it's brave!) to pave the way for others. "So cricket has obviously been a massive part of your life?" I ask, and add, "Do you think it's made you who you are and given you more opportunities?" "Without doubt. If you'd asked people, back when I started playing, 'Will there ever be a female professional umpire?' the answer would have been 'no'. It's only very recently that the opportunities have existed. And my life has definitely changed, my behaviour has changed, my skill-sets have changed as a result of playing a team sport. I'm aware that being involved in adult sports at such a young age has shaped me. I've always been an emotional character, but becoming a cricket umpire has made me more resilient. I've been incredibly lucky to be given these opportunities, and to be part of a special game."

Left to follow other avenues, Sue may well have excelled in badminton or swimming, but if she had done so she wouldn't have been in the front seat of a burgeoning sport, as she is with women's cricket. "Cricket has shaped me since the age of nine," she concludes, "and to see it adapt before my eyes is really special." But there's plenty more to come for Sue. Like me, she loves traditional cricket and would love to be involved in more Test matches. So let's hope for her and for the future of women's cricket, she gets her dream.

Callum Flynn

IN JANUARY 2024 I met up with the journalist Steve Morgan in the wrong pub in London. I wanted to get an idea about disability cricket in this country, and I had chosen the right man. Wrong pub; right man.

Steve, as he put it, is "a fully paid-up member of the disability cricket fan club." He has all the enthusiasm that a newly graduated journalist would have, but with the experience of a man who has done the circuit, and with the wisdom that former knowledge brings with it. When he finally locates me in my version of the Northcote Arms, I ask how he got involved in the world of disability cricket. "I worked for Haymarket where I eventually became features editor on ECB publications, and I discovered disability cricket through work for matchday programmes." It might be his London accent or his casual clothes that convince me that there's something of the maverick about Steve. He doesn't want to follow predictable paths, and he's found, in disability cricket, a cause that he really believes in, one that needs the whole-hearted support that he gives it.

"I think it's the joy with which people play the game, and the way that they treat their triumphs and disappointments in equal measure. It's the purity of spirit that I found was increasingly missing from professional sport, with that chest-beating alpha-male stuff. I'm not saying that doesn't exist within the disability world, but it's not so obvious and it's bloody good cricketers playing at a level of sport I could only have dreamed of as a club cricketer, even in my best days. It's well beyond the capabilities of our first team."

It was through Steve that I was able to find the contacts I needed at the ECB who could tell me more about disability cricket. It's a well-staffed group: Ian Martin, Head of Disability Cricket; Richard Hill, Disability Cricket Competitions Manager; Edgar Herridge, Senior National Disabilities Manager and Neil Bradshaw, Disability Cricket Operations Manager. I spoke to them all and was struck by their genuine enthusiasm surrounding this sector of the game. This may have originated from their surprise at the quality of the cricket, but it's now more to do with the 'purity of spirit' that Steve Morgan identified. All the players have wrestled with their own physical or mental constraints to get where they are. They work together as a support group, but also with a sense of recognition and understanding. There are no obvious allowances made. The game is played in a spirit of positivity and with a determination to compete as a team.

There are so many players with fascinating stories to tell, so many who voice their debt to cricket, that I am spoiled for choice but I end up speaking at length with Callum Flynn, the current captain of the Physical Disability (PD) England Team. We meet at Loughborough University, where the semi-finals of the third year of the Disability Premier League (DPL) are taking place. It is a new addition to the county game and England's disability groups and a very popular one, not least because the final is being televised on Sky ahead of the England v Australia ODI at Cardiff. This is a great chance for me to meet a lot of the players, to get an idea of the skill level and to see for myself the strong bond that links these disabled cricketers.

I arrive at the university in the sort of rain that bounces hard off the ground and creates puddles in a matter of seconds. It is 9 o'clock in the morning, with play due to start at 11. The short walk through Loughborough's impressive sporting facilities leaves me totally sodden. Callum has promised me a seriously good cup of coffee in the indoor centre, and so I make my way there, meeting a welcoming Steve Morgan on the stairs and being introduced to Jane Powell, the impressive Performance Manager of England Disability Cricket. Despite the downpour, the place is buzzing with players. I meet Callum, and we are ushered into an office. There is no chance of immediate play, so I sit down, the promised excellent coffee in hand, to listen to Callum's story.

Callum was very keen on sport as a youngster. He played a bit of everything, he tells me, but cricket was always the main attraction. And yes, he looks very sporty in his DPL hoody and shorts, his short haircut and beard. I wonder whether he has tattoos, but they aren't on show if he does. He looks like the kind of young man who is hung together by energy drinks and a regular gym routine. He is very relaxed and extremely amiable as I start to quiz him, with an easy and impressively professional manner, as though he has talked about himself plenty of times before.

"Was it school, club or family that took you down the cricket path?" I ask him. "Well, mainly my dad more than anything. He was my coach, and he played as well. I was doing well in trampolining and football, but cricket was my real passion, and I was good enough to be part of Lancashire's youth side, until I got sick."

And so, there you have it. A young, fit kid, excelling in sport, suddenly found that he couldn't move his leg. "I was around twelve when I got the first symptoms. I woke up one morning, and my leg was just locked at a 90-degree angle. We were told to go to the walk-in centre. They palmed me off and didn't even do an X-ray. They said they thought it was a viral infection and gave me some pain-relief tablets." "What happened then?" I ask. "I carried on getting it. It would happen for about a week, and then the leg would straighten out again. But then it wouldn't happen again for about three or four months. We kept going back to the walk-in centre, and we kept being told it was just a viral thing. In the end, we went to the doctor, and it took him two minutes. He felt behind my knee, and he knew straight away. I was in Birmingham Orthopaedic Hospital the following week for a biopsy."

It was on his fourteenth birthday that Callum was told that he had bone cancer. "Did you think you were going to die?" I ask, imagining my own reaction. "Obviously I expected the worst and asked that question straight away. I burst into tears, but they told me that they thought that they'd caught it early enough, even though it was eighteen months later than it should have been." It's easy to understand the frustration that those months of misdiagnosis still provoke, and Callum explains, "A lot of people are misdiagnosed, and it can cost them their life. I've done a lot of fund-raising for the Bone Cancer Research Trust, and that was kind of their slogan for a little while: IT JUST TAKES AN X-RAY." We talk for a bit about how important it is to catch these things early, how stretched the NHS staff are and how saving lives can come down to something so simple. Talking with Callum about the NHS and its inadequate funding is a chastening experience, both of us aware of its importance in an inclusive world.

"Had it spread?" I ask. "Luckily, they'd caught it soon enough, and it was just behind my right knee. If it was any higher, I think I'd have had to have an amputation." Callum goes on to explain that he had a titanium knee-replacement with "two rods going into the bones which connect everything. They also thought they would have to take out three or four muscles, because the tumour was attached to them and was kind of killing them, but they only had to take out one when they opened me up." He is trying to put it in layman's terms, but even so I can barely understand the anatomical logic. What I do know, though, is that knee replacements don't last forever, that there's a limit to the number you can have, and that Callum has already had two. "I had to have another one put in when I was seventeen, because it was causing stress fractures. So they took the old one out and put in a new one, and ever since I've had absolutely no problems." And then he says – and this is a common thread among the people I've interviewed – "I've been very lucky, to be honest." Luck is very much in the eye of the beholder, I think to myself, but this attitude is obviously so important in the lives of people who succeed in adversity. There isn't room for self-pity, and you're not going to succeed if you fall into it.

Matt Askin, for example, with whom I talked on Zoom earlier in 2024, shortly after he'd retired from England Disability Cricket, told me, "I don't think I would have been the person that I am if I didn't have the opportunities that disability cricket has afforded me. And I feel very lucky." Matt, born with a congenital defect, was without an arm. His parents decided that, from three months old, he should have a prosthetic arm, and he spent his childhood hyper-conscious of this 'difference'. "I spent a lot of time as a kid wearing long sleeves, and if I crossed my arms, I put my hand over where my socket joined the arm." Matt went on to be a successful and belligerent one-armed batter for England's PD Team. I'll come back to him.

Callum's operation was in July, and what followed was an intensive course of chemotherapy. Perhaps it's maternal instinct, but this tugs deep at me. What a time in a young lad's life to be shot full of poison. It didn't sit well with him either. "I lost my hair, and I dropped down to about four stone because I couldn't eat. I couldn't swallow tablets, and I had to have everything in medicine form, and you know, it's not Calpol, it's not tasting nice." "You must have looked pretty poorly," I say sympathetically, memories of my son at that age plucking at the heart-strings. "Yeah, bald, skinny and a proper load of mouth-ulcers. So yeah, I did struggle on the chemotherapy." Callum explains that he was on the treatment for six to seven months, and in all that time the anti-sickness drugs worked for him for only a single week.

"So that one week, well it was as if I was living like a king, you know, McDonald's and Chinese and everything." When I ask Callum if the treatment made him tired, he acknowledges that it did, but that it was more a case of being poked and prodded all the time. "I was on a hydration drip which meant I had to go to the toilet every two hours, so I was getting up to go to the bathroom, and I had to collect it all in pots, so it was more that I just couldn't relax, being constantly linked up to a machine."

Cancer is tough to get at any age, but when you're a growing and naturally active teenager keen to operate in top gear, to stay in neutral or be forced into reverse must have been tough to deal with, I suggest. "Yeah, but I think in some ways it was easier then because I was young, whereas if I got cancer now that I'm a bit more aware of everything that's going on, I'd have found it a lot harder. When you're young you feel unbreakable." And I agree with him. It makes sense that as a child in his parent's care, he could just obediently turn up and let the doctors do what they had to do without focusing on the wider implications. As he explains, the big words didn't mean much to him. What mattered was that he was just coming up to that crucial point in his education when he had to choose his GCSE options. The school let him do that from the hospital. "They got me into a private room, and said, 'Listen, whatever options you want, you can have. Just tell us now.' So I chose my options ready for the next year. And I went back to school properly in year 10. I missed my mock exams, although they sent me home with some, but I could never settle to do them."

It was when he occasionally had a week off chemo that he was encouraged to go into school – to try and recover some sort of normality, but it was tough to turn up with no hair, as he explains: "One of the things that I remember the most, and I feel sorry for the teacher because I always tell this story. I had a cap on to hide the bald head, and the head teacher had agreed (we weren't supposed to wear hats in school). And I was lining up to go into Maths at the time, and the teacher saw me and said, 'You have to take your cap off.' I said, 'No, I'm allowed to wear it', and he just pulled it off my head. And then he saw the bald head, and I think it kind of clicked with him. Obviously, he felt dreadful because he'd just forgotten or didn't know. But it was the first time that all my mates had seen me looking ill, and it peed them off a little bit. Some of them weren't happy with the teacher. But that's kind of a vivid memory."

Going into school was a good way of getting on with his life, but it was during the weekends, free of treatment, that he was able to focus on one of his greatest passions. He spent his time down at his local cricket club, Swinton, doing the scoring. He was able to lose himself in the familiar atmosphere of the cricket. There was one time, after the second spell of chemotherapy, when his white blood cell levels were so low that he had to stay in an isolation room and have limited visitors. "I only got really ill once, but it was more just the side effects. I had so many ulcers that I couldn't speak, could hardly drink or eat. The only meal I could have was mash and gravy, but even that I was struggling to keep down. I was just sick all the time."

Cricket, and thoughts of his future in it, kept him going through this time. He admits that he "never really listened to the doctors saying that I might not play sport again, because I just didn't want to hear it." Callum was focusing on getting better and returning to playing for Lancashire. Listening to doctors pulling the plug on that dream was too difficult. There's a fine balance between believing in or deceiving yourself. Callum took the correct path for himself; he continued to focus on a future in cricket.

"Thankfully," he tells me, "2009 was an Ashes year and I had all the magazines and papers with the reports to read." Although he wasn't able to watch because the broadcasting was behind a paywall, he was able to mainline on the 2005 box-set edition of that year's wonderful Ashes series. "Because of the number of times I watched it, I could probably recite word-for-word the commentary, like the Simon Jones ball and everything." Cricket, he insists, kept him going through his chemotherapy.

With titanium knee in place, and a ban on contact sport for life, Callum was eventually able to leave hospital with a positive prognosis. He was unable to continue his school trampolining or ever play football again, but cricket, which is considered a non-contact sport, was very much on the cards. It wasn't long, possibly not quite long enough, before he was back in the nets. "I started training as soon as I got off my crutches, got a knee-brace and could stand unaided. My coach was a guy called Ben Johnson, a West Indian. He coaches at the Lancashire indoor centre, and I'd been with him my whole cricketing life." Callum explains that, before his treatment, he used to spend two hours every Saturday in the winter, netting with three or four others. "As soon as I could stand up unaided, I went back, but only on the bowling machine. Just standing there and hitting. That's all I did. I just stood there and hit balls." "And did you do that because you wanted to normalise your life a little bit?" I ask. "Yes, I did, but also it was just the love that I had for cricket. It was so clear in my mind that it was the sport I wanted to play."

At this point I ask him the question that must have been hard for him to confront. "Were you hoping that you'd continue where you left off?" "Yeah," he admits. "I was probably still a bit blinded because I was so young, and I was thinking I could still make it. There was one coach, when Ben wasn't there one week, who said, 'Look, you're coming back too soon. You know, you shouldn't be playing.' And I was a bit like, 'Let me decide when. You're not going through this. Just let me do whatever I need to do, even though I might be coming back too soon. I'm only training. I'm not playing the game; I'm not costing anyone a match'. So, you know, you still had comments from people."

Callum had been in hospital for the best part of a year, then a further nine months in recovery, so he'd lost nearly two years of his childhood or, as he puts it, "I'd missed socialising with my friends and formative cricket training. At that age you are starting to take sport a bit more seriously and seeing if you can make something of yourself." He was obviously very driven, more focused than most others of his age, probably partly because of what he'd been through.

The following season Callum was back on the pitch, playing in the league. "Because I couldn't run at the time, the league asked all the clubs if they minded if I had a runner, explaining the situation. Everyone agreed." He shrugs as he tells me that most people were great about it, but there was always someone who made a comment, someone who didn't understand. "And this was when you were about fifteen?" I ask. "Yes," he replies. "I was just playing third-team club cricket, no Lancashire cricket because obviously I couldn't run. Then someone mentioned disability cricket to me." To Callum, who was desperately trying to forget about the cancer and get on with his life as though it hadn't happened, this wasn't a serious proposition, not one he wanted to think about. "As a young kid, you know, you sort of have a bit more pride, and you think, I've just been training for Lancashire, I'm not disabled. I don't want to play for a disabled team – because you instantly think of wheelchairs."

Callum isn't the only disabled cricketer to feel this way. Labels often conjure up negative images, and those that arise from the word 'disabled' surely can't be readily welcomed by a young sportsman.

Matt Askin had a similar response when the suggestion was made to him. "I was taken aback a bit, but I went to watch a disabled cricket game and found that it wasn't taking the mick. There were some legitimately good cricketers, far better than I was, and people who were embracing their disability and using it to their advantage. One thing that stood out for me was the Shropshire wicket-keeper, Dave Ingram. He was in a wheelchair, and he took a catch by diving out of his chair, and I thought he is fully embracing everything about the game, and I thought I can get on board with this." Matt went on to play for the Shropshire Disability Team, and as luck would have it found he was in the right place at the right time. England was getting a disability team together, and Matt was there at its formation. He remained in the England team for thirteen years until he retired in 2023.

Like Matt, Callum went to have a look at some disability cricket. "I thought it would be a bit gentler, with a few boundaries here and there. But no, there was a guy who was blasting the ball everywhere." Callum went for a net, and a few weeks later he was in the Lancashire disability team, playing against a Yorkshire side which included the opening batter for England's PD team. "I did okay, got 40 odd and, unbeknown to me, the batter had messaged the England coach and said, 'There's a player here that you need to get on the team.' And I got a letter through from the ECB inviting me to England trials."

For Callum, the barriers he'd built up against disability cricket had come down. He was no longer thinking 'disability'. He had his eyes on 'England cricket'. This was a big mindset-change, and Callum was open enough to understand the opportunity suddenly presented to him. "I would probably never have had the chance to play for England before but now, because of my disability, and not despite it, I had been given that possibility." It's still there, the wide-eyed excitement, as he describes to me receiving his ECB letter. He went to Malvern for a weekend's trial, and then he was selected to play for the England PD Team against the Army at Bournville. Jonathan Trott, Chris Tremlett and Mike Gatting were there watching. "It was a bit of a pinch-me moment, with my family there, too. I got a few runs as well, so it was quite a good day. And we won. A proper dream-come-true moment. I did quite a lot of interviews. People asking how I felt, and it was hard to answer because I was there living the dream."

Callum just wants to keep embracing the opportunity and enjoying his cricket. He is unfailingly grateful for the chance to play for England that he has been given. And this is true of all the England disabled cricketers that I talk to. Jonathan Gale, who plays for England Learning Disability Team (LD) tells me that, "Cricket's just always been my sort of motivation and kind of happy place in life."

Jonathan, who now has a job as a cricket coach, going into schools on behalf of Surrey CCC, is autistic. He tells me that, "Cricket has really helped me to channel my autism and turn it into a positive tool, using cricket as a coping mechanism. Like everything you have a bad day, and you hit a ball hard to get that anger out of you. I just used it that way initially." Being part of a cricket team made up of people with similar needs enabled him to channel his autistic traits into his sport. "There's a common thread in the spectrum which is actually quite interesting, because you have players who are quite high-functioning and have full-time jobs. Some have families and are married. And then you've got players who might not have that privilege or life-style, who don't have a wife and a family but will still be able to live independently with available support, so it's incredibly diverse, but it's amazing how, despite the differences, we can all relate to one another, and cricket itself does more of the talking than our impairments." This is quite an insight, and it's clear that Jonathan has had a lot of time to reflect on the benefits that cricket has provided for him.

Callum is quick to highlight the impressive quality of disability cricket. "It's such a good standard, you know. I play cricket in the Greater Manchester Premier League, and so do a lot of the other PD lads. Premier League cricket is a great standard, and disability cricket is right up there. It's a constant battle to convince others that it's not just wheelchair cricket. But now that people like Steve Morgan have seen it and got so mesmerised by it, then hopefully people will start to understand its value. He's one of the biggest advocates for the game." And I'm bound to agree with him, I have rarely seen anyone else quite as starry-eyed about anything as Steve is about disability cricket. And to judge from the people I've talked to, it's clear that he's not alone. "Do the players in the league treat you differently?" I ask Callum. "No, I play in the same side as Jordan Williams, who also plays for the England PD team, and we're treated the same as everyone else." Naturally, you get the odd idiot, Callum admits, but generally they are seen as 'England' players, not 'disabled' ones.

Conscious that we're running out of time and that the sun is now fully out, I ask him quickly about the DPL. "I'm a big advocate for it because I think it's just brilliant in terms of something different. You have the Learning Disability teams, Physical Disability teams and the Deaf teams all mixed up into four squads, with sixteen players in each: the Black Cats, the Hawks (Callum's squad), the Pirates and the Tridents." It shows my ignorance when I ask him if the PD players have the most difficulties. "I think we're the strongest. I mean, I feel a bit big-headed saying that, but I think we are the strongest side, and that might be because we've been through probably tougher journeys, some of us thinking at one stage that we're never going to play sport again, or that we're not going to be here for long. So I feel like it might be the resilience that we've all got. If we come across a little barrier, we're not afraid to try and get over it. And we built that resilience up over our lives and our stories."

"Who is the worst affected by their disability in your group?" I ask. "Probably Fred Bridges. He has cerebral palsy, which has affected the right side of his body. His wrist is fully locked. He's a fantastic left-arm off-spinner, but when we play him, we have to hide him at fine leg or on the 45, because he can only pick up one-handed so it's tough to pick up cleanly. So obviously, we kind of play to that when we play against him," Callum says, laughing. "You have to have a sense of humour. With prosthetic limbs in the changing room, there's a few jokes like 'I can lend a hand' etc."

Before we end, I ask Callum whether he gets paid for playing for England. "No, we don't get paid, but you get your travel expenses, and this year Masuri are providing all the kit for us. This January we went to India, where we performed well and were beaten 3-2, but it was the first tour where we got a small touring fee – £1,000." It was a drop in the ocean for Callum, who is a self-employed builder. He had to take two weeks off work, which meant a genuine loss of earnings. This isn't a straightforward choice, because he is now a mortgage-payer with a young family. "The fee certainly helped, and I believe there are plans to keep increasing it." At twenty-nine, Callum thinks he's unlikely to benefit personally from this, but he is understandably delighted by the direction of travel. "Thankfully, you know the world's going that way. All these lads in the DPL can take advantage of that. We have Jane Powell working with us, who obviously worked with the England women's team as well, and you know we relate ourselves to the England women, because they've been very much on the same journey that we have in terms of striving for recognition."

The previous weekend, Callum tells me, he had to drive from Lancashire to Arundel to play a T20 game, then drive back on the same day. He then had to go to work on the Monday. He didn't get paid for his trip, but he got his fuel. It's a similar story to that of the women, tales of doing their own washing, travelling to far ends of the country and being out of pocket. "We have a lot of respect for them because they have been been there and done it. We take a bit of inspiration that one day disability cricket can get to the same stage they're at."

Women's disabled cricket is still a way behind, but there are plenty of plans afoot. Richard Hill at the ECB has been behind the scenes in disability cricket for thirty years. He has worked with the Lord's Taverners on all levels of provision for disabled people across the country. He is delighted with the recent steps forward but is aware that there is still a lot of progress to be made, especially, he says, in the women's game. "There is work going on around developing a Women's DPL at the moment as well, but it's still a bit embryonic at the moment."

Callum's reference to the history of women's cricket had set me thinking. By the end of our conversation it was positively roasting in our office. Loughborough's state-of-the-art facilities and the hard work of the ground-staff have made the square fit for play to start shortly after lunch, so I have time to catch some of the cricket. It's been a while since I've been at a T20 tournament, and although it doesn't have the crowds or the atmosphere of the T20 Blast Finals Day, there is something unique about the event. It's as though we are 'the lucky few' there to witness the progress of a tournament on the verge of explosive success. I join a family on an available deckchair and settle down to watch The Hawks take on the Tridents. The family are seasoned supporters, and their knowledge of the players is helpful to me. They fill in details about the Hawks, for whom their son plays. The younger sister, obviously a cricketer herself, is frustrated by their batting as they only manage a meagre 31-8, the game having been curtailed by the morning's rain to a five-over thrash. Sadly, Callum doesn't make it out of single figures but the Tridents reach the necessary target and the Hawks' second game is reduced to a battle for third place.

Unfortunately, I need to leave before the final and I head to the station, leaving behind me the hubbub of happy cricketers chattering and cheering, carrying with me a conviction that Callum's life in cricket is working well, and he is at one with the world. His cancer took him on a different path from the one he would otherwise have trodden, but who can say that, despite its cruel origin, it was a worse one? His words echo in my head as I mull over our chat.

"Cricket has given me so much. I'm talking cricket every day. I'm watching cricket at every opportunity. I went straight into working with my dad after university, and then we got the house and the little one. For the moment cricket coaching just doesn't quite match the mortgage, so I can't quite afford that pay-cut yet. I have to put coaching on the back burner for the present, but my dream job would be to coach the England PD team in the future, when I have to give up playing. I'd love to help from the other side of the fence and still be an advocate for disability sport and try to make an impression somewhere along the line. That's what cricket has given me, a sense of hope."

I think about my initial chat with Steve Morgan and realise he wasn't wrong. These lads are playing cricket for the right reasons. If the rise and rise of the cult cricketer towards the mercenary in mainstream cricket topples into grim reality, the sense of team spirit and togetherness in the disability game is like a breath of fresh air.

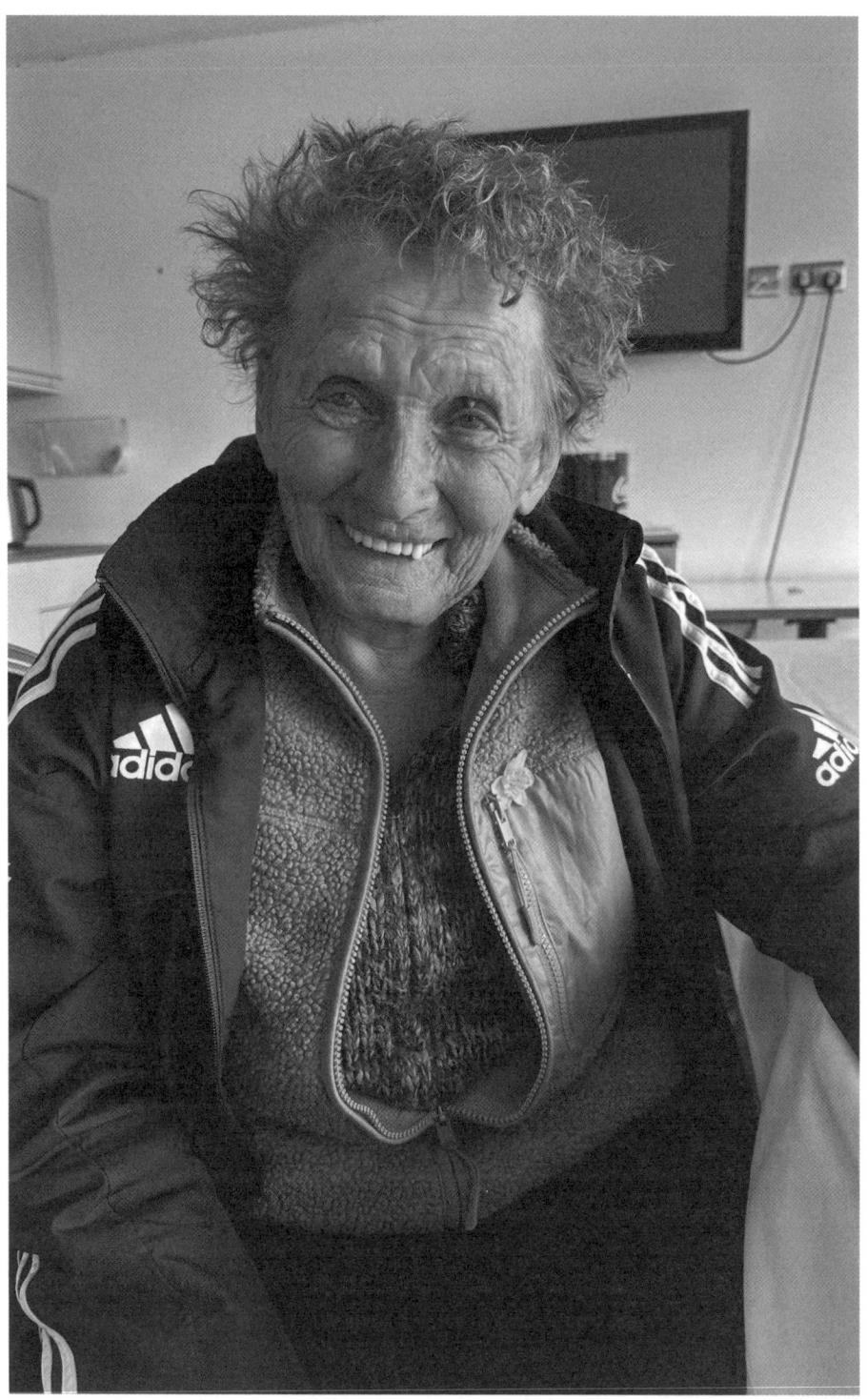

Enid Bakewell

ENID BAKEWELL IS CONSIDERED THE BEST-EVER ENGLISH ALL-ROUNDER in women's cricket. In Tests, she scored 1,078 runs (12 Tests and 23 ODIs) at an average of 59.88 with four centuries, while taking 50 wickets at an average of 16.62. She scored an unbeaten 112 and took 10 for 75 in a match against West Indies at Edgbaston in 1979. She was the first England woman to score 100 runs and take 10 wickets in the same Test. In 2012, she was the third woman to be inducted into the ICC Cricket Hall of Fame (after Rachael Heyhoe Flint and Belinda Clark).'

It lays bare the invisibility of the women's game that someone of Enid Bakewell's talent remains relatively unknown, even to a knowledgeable cricket community. She is, in fact, as unforgettable as she is likeable, with a cheeky, conspiratorial charm that immediately puts you at ease. She's hard to pin down, not because she is unwilling, more because she is still very much in demand. Enid, in her mid-eighties, is a very active woman, and it wasn't straightforward to organise a time and place for our meeting. Conveniently for me, it is at Somerset's home ground in Taunton that we finally meet, during a rain-break (that proved terminal) in the women's one-day international between England and Pakistan in May 2024.

I find Enid in the Member's Pavilion holding court at a table of women cricketers and media. It is the aftermath of a lunch long since finished, and post-prandial spirits are high. She'd sent me an email shortly before: 'Hi there youngster Annie, are you at the Taunton cricket ground? I am here in the toilet as it's raining hard yet again. I do not think that they will be able to get back to play. We could meet up. Please text me. Lots of love ExBx'. I feel bad leading her away from such a convivial occasion, but she just laughs and says, "They'll be glad to see me go." I doubt that somehow.

We manage to commandeer a comfortable hospitality suite for an hour so I sit opposite her and begin to ask her about her life. The window is open, so that the rain and the announcer provide a soundtrack to the interview. On our way over, I wince at the number of steps needed, but Enid seems unfazed, an attitude that is very much part of her charm. She is, in old-fashioned terms, a 'trooper', nothing too much bother, eternally cheerful.

Enid (née Turton) was born in 1940 in Newstead, a village created in 1875 to serve the mining industry in the heart of Nottinghamshire's coalfields. It was a company village, occupied by local miners and their families, and it was normal for families to occupy the houses for a few years before graduating to Newstead's 'new town', built in the 1920s. "The new houses were semi-detached and boasted an indoor toilet," Enid explains to me. "The old houses were terraced, and they had to go across the backyard to get to the toilet." This inconvenience didn't affect Enid's family though, since, for reasons unknown to her, her father had managed to move straight to the 'new town'.

Enid's fiercely socialist roots are evident the minute she begins to talk about Newstead, and it's easy to understand why. '60 years ago, when young Enid Turton lived in Newstead, there was a colliery – one of the highest producing in the country – and a significant railway junction where three lines came together', Simon Sweetman writes in his biography, *Enid Bakewell: Coalminer's Daughter*. Today, Enid explains, there is no sign of the industry that was so vital to the community she grew up in, a community that was decimated by the pit closures which began in the 80s, the last of them closing in 2015.

"I was an only," she tells me, when I ask about her childhood. "My parents had lost somebody earlier, so Mum was 40 when I was born. I was a real tomboy. I had these lovely plaits and curls that my mother used to get a great kick out of, but I didn't like. If I went to school and undid one of them, she'd know immediately." It was in secondary school that Enid discovered there were people who cut hair! "And I went and had it cut off without telling my mother," she laughs. "In what way were you a tomboy?" I ask. "I was only interested in mucking about and playing sport. I wanted to play cricket with the boys." It's apparent that, although her parents weren't sporty, they were supportive of this 'rebellion', as she goes on to explain. "They didn't give me pocket money, but they bought me all the cricket equipment that I wanted. I had the bat and the stumps, wicket-keeping gloves and the ball, and so the boys always called on me to go and play." "Why did they get you cricket things?" I ask. "That's what I wanted," she tells me simply. "I liked cricket, and I enjoyed playing it. I used to go and watch the men on the cricket pitch because it was a mining area, so everybody who lived there was a miner, and I knew them." The cricket pitch in this instance was the Colliery Recreation Ground.

Enid played her cricket on a long road that led up to the railway station. "We used an electricity box as our wicket." She maintains that her street cricket taught her how to play straight, because "if you hit it to the side it would go into somebody's garden, and you'd end up losing the ball." They moved on to a field by the vicarage where the boys kept hitting the ball into the garden in order to scrump apples from the vicar's tree, she explains, but the cricket was paramount. When they had to abandon that field, they found a way to continue playing. "Every year, for a few weeks, the ponies that worked in the pit were given time to graze on the field, and so we were moved on, and we got down on our hands and knees and cut a pitch with scissors and shears in an old disused field by the cemetery." It's not uncommon that such humble beginnings help to form a cricketing style, and Enid is quick to point out that "you didn't let it bounce, as you didn't know where it was going to go, so it taught me to move my feet and hit the ball before it bounced. That and the horrible things that we found in the long grass," she adds. If they did lose the ball, which happened regularly, her mum often came to help look for it. It was Enid's ball after all! Rachael Heyhoe Flint backed up Enid's theory about the origins of her idiosyncratic footwork. "I always reckoned," she wrote, "that the rather unkempt nature of Enid's village pitch taught her to use her feet rather than letting the ball bounce. Adept footwork was the hallmark of her batting; she would skip down the wicket, even in her first over at the crease, regardless of the status of the game."

Enid's dad Len never had a chance to pursue his own chosen career. "He wanted to teach," Enid says, "but he was one of eight boys, so he had to go down the mine like the rest. He was over the moon when I took up teaching." He was a mine deputy and shot-firer (breaking rocks into manageable sizes for mineral extraction), working at Newstead Colliery for over 40 years, she tells me. He worked night-shifts, which meant that Enid was encouraged to play outside in the daytime, so as not to disturb him. He was also a terribly proud union man, who became a local councillor. The origins of Enid's Labour Party activism can clearly be seen in her father's support of his working-class colleagues and comrades.

Enid attended the local grammar school, Brincliffe, "which was later closed down by Maggie Thatcher," she says with a glint in her eye. It was there that she was introduced to club cricket. "The PE teacher knew somebody who played in a cricket team in Nottingham," she explains. Keen to get involved, when she was twelve, Enid used to go to the University of Nottingham every week to play in the nets. "There were lots of pitches where we used to play cricket and then hockey in the winter. I'd get my homework done and then I'd go down there. I really loved it, and of course I was reasonably good because I'd practised for so long. I used my feet really well." At this early stage, Enid found she was getting mixed advice from coaches and others. "Some people," she tells me, "told me to take it slowly and don't let them push you too soon." Others would tell her to ignore these cautions. 'You're talented, so you should play and go with the flow,' they'd say. It appeared that everyone wanted a piece of her because she possessed the perfect combination to succeed. Her talent was evident, and she clearly had the drive and enthusiasm to play as often as she could.

Enid made her debut for Nottinghamshire when she was just fourteen. "To begin with, I got into the county team batting at number seven. But then I got moved up, and I was batting at the top." Netta Rheinberg, the cricketer and journalist, wrote about Enid's early years in the 1970 *Wisden*:

At fourteen Enid had already graduated from her club to her county team. In those days she was a quiet, steady, right-hand opening bat, concentrating on staying at the wicket. The lessons of concentration and watchfulness learnt in those early years provided a solid basis for the future, as she found later, when the opportunity arose, that she was not only able to stay at the wicket, but also to score easily.

Many of the games she played for Nottingham CC were against Nottingham Casuals, who were their big rivals. We talk briefly about the number of teams there were and how much travel was required. "We played against Leicester as well, but most games we had to travel a long way. Lynne Thomas, who played for Glamorgan, I remember she had to travel sixty miles just to do a net during the week." It's hard to imagine today the dedication required from players who had to travel that far just for a net, let alone the distances to games, home as well as away, with only a limited number of teams around the country. Women were playing a good level of cricket despite the minimal recognition they received. Even with the foundation of the Women's Cricket Association in 1926, and the publication of *Women's Cricket*, a magazine published by the WCA from 1930 to 1967, it's an eternal frustration for those trying to piece together the history of women's cricket that so many early scorecards are either incomplete or missing. It wasn't until Enid's era that their value began to be fully recognised. It is clear from the records available, that even at such a young age Enid was starting to make a name for herself. It wasn't long before she was playing for the Midlands, still only sixteen years old.

In 1959, her final year of school, Enid was picked for the WCA team to play in Holland, where they had to play on matting. "I was successful with my bowling," she tells me, "but I didn't really get a chance to bat there." It was unlucky for her that there was a bit of a hiatus in international women's cricket in 1960, and that in 1961, because of illness due to a poor diet, she was not able to join England's tour of South Africa. But it had been important to dip her toes in an international career at such a young age and was a sign of what was to come in the not-too-distant future. For the present, though, Enid had a fair amount to deal with at home. She passed her A Levels, and then, during her time at school, she got engaged to Douglas Bradshaw, a neighbour.

She was successful in her teacher training application and went on to attend Dartford. "What was it like?" I ask her. "They had a cricket pitch and a deputy principal who played for England." This makes me laugh and we talk briefly about her priorities. Clearly they were cricket, I suggest. Enid goes on to tell me that the Deputy Principal was Mary Duggan, England's captain at that time. "She was a quick bowler who could bat as well; a big, tall lady. Before I knew what she played like, I went to field against her and I was standing really close, and a woman at slip suggested, 'I'd go a bit further back if I were you, as she really smashes them'. And I soon ended up on the boundary and still managed to drop the ball when she hit it to me." It wasn't only Mary Duggan who stood out and encouraged all the Dartford cricketers. Ruth Westbrook, later Prideaux, who kept wicket for England, also taught there. Dartford had a reputation for producing England cricketers, and Enid was part of a strong intake, including Mary Pilling, Jackie Elledge, Sandra Brown, Ann Jago, Mollie Hunt and the future England captain, Rachael Heyhoe Flint, who was a couple of years above Enid. They had known each other through the county scene, when Rachael played for Staffordshire, but it was at Dartford that they became friends.

Enid seems to have followed the perfect route into cricket, as well as into teaching. She found herself near the centre of women's cricket, she was getting known and was in demand. Representing a number of high-profile sides, she was inevitably seen by leading members of the WCA. "It can't have been easy," I suggest, "to play for various teams and to study full-time." Enid admits that it got complicated. "I was teaching in Surrey, so of course there was a conflict because Surrey wanted me to play for them – so I did for a bit – but then I went back to play for the Midlands." She completed her Dartford course although it wasn't a qualification in the same sense as today, she explains. "You got a certificate to say that you'd studied for three years, and that was all." In 2017, Enid was awarded – for the work she'd done at Dartford – a degree from Greenwich University. "It was a great honour," she says.

As well as completing her teacher training, Enid benefited from some very useful cricketing input. "I started to concentrate properly on my bowling and was being coached by Eileen White and Edna Valentine, who were part of the County Association," she explains. With them, she worked hard at creating a bowling style. "I modelled my left-arm spin bowling on Tony Lock. I even had the same number of steps in my run-up." These were formative years that built on her early experience and turned her into a successful all-rounder. As I talk to her, it's easy to see, behind those bright eyes, the determination needed to succeed: a willpower that saw her practising endlessly on her run-up, searching for that extra edge.

Following in the footsteps of Heyhoe Flint, Enid was soon 'on the books' for England. But this coincided with her 'off the cricket-ground' life, which was progressing quickly as well. Douglas had left Enid in her third year at Dartford, moving to Australia and marrying another woman. Enid admitted to Sweetman that it was probably on the rebound from Doug that Enid quickly got engaged again, this time to Colin Bakewell. It was a whirlwind engagement, with today's conventional wisdom probably suggesting that she was young and headstrong.

Having qualified as a PE teacher, she got her first job, in January 1963, at Sherwood Hall Business School for Girls, and she wed Colin in 1964. Marriage took her away from her home in Newstead to the nearby Annesley Woodhouse, which, as Enid is keen to point out, "had a chip shop opposite providing lunch on Saturdays." Lorna, their first child, was born in 1966. It wasn't long before she was juggling the responsibilities of a busy family life with playing cricket as often as she could.

Enid missed England selection when New Zealand toured England in 1966, as Lorna was born at the end of the season. There were stories of her playing club cricket when five months pregnant, but there was no chance of her being chosen for that series. But in 1967 Enid kept fit and played as often as she could, maintaining her form. "I would read Lorna a story and then put on my training gear and go outside. On the pavement I would wait until a car approached and I would attempt to race it past two lights. Then I would go back and repeat the process." This wholehearted dedication resulted in her being asked to tour with England to Australia in 1968. This was a big break, one she had coveted, but there was the matter of leaving a young family. "Was it a tough decision?" I ask. "It wasn't easy," she replies. "But my family were really supportive, and they persuaded me to go, even though it meant four months away." Her parents would help look after Lorna, and besides, they told her, it would only get harder as she got older. The decision was made, but it wasn't straightforward financially. Not only did it mean four months away, but Enid had to raise the £600 for the flights. "I had to set up a stall and sell things like fruit and vegetables from my dad's allotment, as well as books and anything I could make." Enid sold these in the village and managed to reach the target – this miner's daughter from Nottinghamshire was going to Australia to play for the Ashes.

What strikes me more than anything else, when talking to Enid, is just how much she wanted to play cricket. It certainly wasn't for money – in fact quite the opposite. It was because she loved it. Her determination to play, despite the obvious barriers, shows a love of the game that is at the heart of her success. Playing for the love of playing shouldn't be unusual, but with the modern game so embroiled in cult status, franchise wages and the creating of mega-rich mega-stars, this attitude appears to be in danger of disappearing. She was one of the few married tourists and, I think, the only mother, and she had the guilt and the stresses that come with those roles. It says a lot about Enid and her team-mates, and also about the era, that they played despite the cost, and not for the reward. In no way am I endorsing the appalling lack of payment, recognition and the ridiculous conditions that the women had to deal with, but something has been lost both in the men's and women's game, with the passing of such generous commitment. Enid and I discuss what cricket means to her, and she doesn't falter on this. "It made me who I am."

Enid is too modest to tell me how she got on in Australia and New Zealand on that first tour, but Rachael Heyhoe Flint wrote that, "Enid's performance on that 1968/69 Australasian tour was so outstanding that she became the first woman cricketer – after 75 years of women's Test cricket – to be featured in *Wisden*, a five-page spread no less." Enid's figures back this up. On her first Test appearance she reached her highest score of 113, and in the 11 matches that she played in Australia she amassed 53 wickets with her left-arm spin at an average of 11.8. In the Australian press, she was the 'English girl who does a Sobers' and, more patronisingly, 'She played like a man'. When she was complimented on her 'orthodox left-arm spin that was bowled with consistency and good drift', her typically forthright comment was, "Spin bowlers were only as good as the batsmen make them look."

When she returned, Nottingham gave her a civic reception, headed by the mayor. Enid thinks it was a Labour council at the time, but she can't remember the details. It would have been a proud moment for her parents. I wonder if they understood the significance of her entry into the *Wisden Almanack* the following year. She is not sure they did. Another, more financially rewarding, result of her sparkling performance, was the beginning of a sponsorship deal. Rachael Heyhoe Flint records it:

Enid's first personal 'sponsorship in kind' came as a result of her high sporting profile in her native county after her triumphs Down Under in '68 and '69. Reg Simpson, the Nottinghamshire and England legend who represented Gunn and Moore, saw a photo of Enid wielding a rather ancient version of one of their bats, held together with black adhesive tape. Reg invited Enid to visit Gunn and Moore's showroom and choose a new bat. Thus began a very happy sponsorship partnership.

"What a fantastic start to your England career," I say, and Enid agrees. Trying to get her to assess her own performance I ask her how happy she was with how she did. She diverts the conversation by concentrating on her opening partner, Lynne Thomas, and how they worked well as a pair. "You should be interviewing Lynne," she tells me. "She was a great player, and we worked hard together to forge a good opening partnership." I had met Lynne briefly when I'd stolen Enid from her table of friends, and Enid makes many references to her. It's obvious that they are still very much in touch, as well as having been a thoroughly successful opening pair for England.

After the plaudits following the Antipodean tour, there was a dearth of international women's cricket, and during the enforced break in cricket Enid had two more children in quick succession. Lynne, born in January 1970 (and named after her opening partner), and Robert, unplanned in September 1971. Sadly, just after Lynne's birth, Enid learned that her mother had breast cancer. "She delayed telling me or visiting a doctor for so long that by the time she saw anyone it was too late." Enid explains that her parents never fully cottoned on to the NHS. "To them, it cost to see the doctor, and there was a genuine fear of hospitals." It was guilt, that age-old curse of the female sex, that she remembers feeling more than anything else. "I wasn't able to be there for her as much as I would have liked because of having two small children, and she kept it from me so as not to worry me." Enid was only thirty-one when her mother died. Now, she had not only three young children, but also a recently widowed father, to care for.

Being a woman cricketer wasn't ever going to be plain sailing. Despite her early success, Enid needed to stay in the spotlight to be in contention for national cricket, to keep her foot in the door. Partly because of this, and partly because, as she tells me, she saw no reason not to play, pregnancy didn't keep her out of county cricket. As Simon Sweetman writes, she was six months pregnant when she took 8 for 53 'in a marathon spell for East Midlands against East Anglia'. (The Midlands had been split into two teams, East Midlands – Enid's team – and West Midlands).

Unsurprisingly, Enid was part of the national team for the inaugural Women's World Cup which was held in England in 1973. This was a tournament that preceded the men's and provided it with a template. It was spearheaded and sponsored by Jack Hayward, son of millionaire industrialist Charles Hayward. Rachael Heyhoe Flint, who was an accomplished fundraiser, credited Jack with coming up with the idea "over a bottle of rum". In her autobiography *Heyhoe!*, she writes:

Someone once asked him, a little scathingly, why he ploughed so much of his money into women's cricket. 'It's quite simple,' he replied. 'I love women, and I love cricket – and what could be better than to have the two rolled together?'

Jack Hayward obviously had a lot of time for Rachael, as he was very supportive of her plans and her fundraising, providing financial support for several women's tours.

Enid began her one-day international career in the same way as she had her Test career. She scored a century, 101 not out. England reached the final against Australia, and Enid again had a big impact, helping the side to victory with an impressive 118. "It was a great event to be part of," she tells me. In a rare moment of evident pride, and without my prompting, she adds, "Unlike others, who looked where the fielders were, I would look where the spaces were and try to hit the ball into those spaces." A key difference? Whatever it was, whether it was finding the spaces or using her feet, Enid, a young mother, was making a significant impact with both bat and ball, topping the tournament batting with an average of 88, and contributing a not-to-be-scoffed-at 4 wickets for 91 from 30 overs.

It's hard to see how, with three children and a widowed father, she was able to find the time to play cricket. Enid makes much of the fact that she was an only child, and it was probably at this time that the lack of siblings was most evident. Nonetheless she continued to find time for cricket. She was appointed captain of East Midlands in 1972 and made her life a lot more complicated in 1974 when she went back into work. "I got a job as a swimming teacher in a learner pool that was attached to my girls' primary school. It was a fabulous job, but the pool was affected by mining subsidence, so I had to put on a costume each day and examine the area to see if there were any cracks. There were also steps to enter the pool, and they were wide, which made it possible for me to let the children pretend they were crocodiles, so that they got their heads wet – which is the basis of being able to swim." That makes sense to me. Images of my own swimming instructor at my primary school flash in front of my eyes, and I tell her how the terrifying woman used a long pole with a hook on it to scoop out anyone not listening. Enid must have been a fabulous teacher in comparison, I tell her. "I was definitely delighted to go back to work," she admits, and she tells me how she took Robert along with her. "I made sure that he could swim straight away, so that he would be safe." It was a good job too by all accounts, and Enid was able to make the best of it by increasing her number of hours and pupils. "It was paid hourly, so I worked at weekends and ran night classes too, teaching adults and children." She also worked in the holidays, only stopping when selected to play cricket. "It must have been a buoyant community," I joke, but semi-seriously. I tell her that I can imagine a whole village of enthusiastic swimmers, and

I suggest that the way she transformed a role to take in the whole community helps to illustrate just what a whole-hearted person she is. "I loved it," she says, shrugging off my compliment, "but it was an extremely hot and humid place to work, with temperatures up to 86 degrees. So I got very tired."

In the 1970s, there was plenty of cricket for Enid to be part of – and not just playing. She became the Junior Organiser for East Midlands, securing a youth coaching certificate with the NCA. "I really enjoyed helping with the young 'uns'," she says, but she had her own cricket career to maintain. When Australia came over in 1976, she was Heyhoe Flint's vice-captain, and she played a big part in England's securing of three draws. Plenty of cricket there might have been, but it was a difficult time for both Enid and Rachael. The WCA dropped Rachael as captain in 1977, giving the role to Mary Pilling. In *Heyhoe!*, Rachael, still obviously deeply hurt by the decision which seemed to her to come from no obvious reason other than she had become 'too big for her boots', described in detail being called into the office and told by Audrey Winterbottom, Chair of the Selectors, that she was no longer captain.

"Can you tell me why?" "It's a committee decision," she replied formally. "Is it anything to do with my playing form?" I ventured, knowing that logically it couldn't be. "No." "In that case, is it anything I've done off the field?" "I can't be specific. I cannot point to 'A' or 'B'. It's a committee decision."

Considering how successful she had been as a captain and given the respect she had in the dressing-room, it did seem a strange and underhand way of going about replacing her. Neither Rachael nor Enid went to India in 1977. Enid's reason was domestic. Rachael was dropped.

Following a National Selection Weekend in 1978, both Enid and Rachael were back in the team that took on the West Indies in 1979. Enid starred in the second Test at Trent Bridge with an unbeaten century and 10 wickets in the match. She was a vital all-rounder for England, but, at nearly forty, she was coming towards the end of her international career. The 1978 World Cup had been a very low-key affair, and Enid had not attended. The 1982 World Cup was to take place in New Zealand, and the teams played seventeen games in less than a month, with sides from Australia, India, England, New Zealand and an International XI taking part. It concluded with a tight final between England and a victorious Australia. Enid was still making important contributions, but there were new players to catch the eye. She continued to play domestically, interspersed with summer coaching of children and a couple of ill-conceived tours of Apartheid South Africa in 1983 and 1985 with the Unicorns. In his book, Sweetman explains that unlike the men's tours, women's cricket went very much under the radar. The difference being was that the women were 'not having their mouths stuffed with krugerrands, but like the men, they played only against all white teams.' Enid explained to him that, 'Basically we wanted to keep women's cricket alive out there.'

There was unrest at home as well as in South Africa, that directly affected Enid and the community around Newstead. The miners' strike had a big impact in Nottingham, with the union at odds with much of the rest of the country. "My dad was a big union man," she explains. "It was an incredibly difficult time, with so much ill feeling and unrest." Enid tells me that, together with the post-Beeching reduction of railway services, the closure of the mines was crippling for Newstead in particular and for Nottinghamshire at large.

In 1990 her father died at the age of 92. He had been a constant in Enid's life, accompanying and driving her to cricket matches and helping with the children. In a role reversal, Enid had spent much of his later life helping him out at his home, cleaning and cooking for him. "Dad had been around for all of my cricket, and I spent a lot of time with him at his allotment and then at his house." Following his death, Enid suffered what can only be described as a bit of a breakdown. She set about repairing his house with the help of her son, Robert. "He lives there now, as I could not cope after my dad died. I just wanted to see him sat with his cat on his knees in front of the fire." It was soon after that that she left Colin, explaining that "at first I didn't know how set in his ways he was. His mother worked in a cigar factory, and so Colin, his dad and sister Beryl drank and smoked. Colin didn't go to the pub or club opposite. He went to a nearby shop to ask them to fill up his bottle with beer. He would then spend the evening watching TV, drinking and smoking. I didn't smoke or drink alcohol, as my parents married in a Methodist Chapel, so I would stay in the dining room to do the paperwork and sort out bills. Then I would put on a classical record, turn out the light and relax. Colin would then come in and say, 'What are you doing in here?' I realised that we'd grown apart." When Nottinghamshire Council was taken over by the Conservative Party, they cut the amount of money available for teaching swimming, and the fact that Colin bought the *Telegraph* for his puzzles started to really rankle. Enid explained that "the cut in swimming lessons meant that my wages were lower, and so I said to Colin that if he bought the *Telegraph*, he would have to give me more house-keeping money to make up for my loss of wages." It was, it seems, time to declare the marriage over.

With her children grown and her father no longer around, in 1993 Enid moved to London, where, as she tells me, "An opportunity arose that I couldn't ignore. A very clever lady, Jenny Wostrack, was promoting women's cricket in schools. I went to help her out. It wasn't an easy task, as some of the schools were in very deprived areas. In some cases, there was broken glass in the playground and parents shouting and swearing at their children. But it was extremely rewarding." It didn't take long, alongside this demanding job, for her to start playing for the Surrey County side, "I had to join the Second XI first, but later I played for the first team." She also played for a well-known side, The Redoubtables, in the Southern Premier League. Cricket was still the mainstay of her life, and she had many roles within the game, including coaching, promoting, writing and playing. In 1996, Enid was given the job of coaching the Under-21's England side, a job which involved travelling with them to South Africa.

Enid, of course, was still playing. In 2001, she went with the MCC to the Netherlands and, as Simon Sweetman points out, this was an impressive 44 years after she first travelled abroad on a cricket tour. And yes, she is still playing. She sent me a message at the end of September 2024, telling me that they'd just played the last game of their season. It doesn't come as easily as it used to, she admits. "I look upon cricket nowadays as a challenge for which I need to keep fit. So I go to Keep Fit class on Monday and Tuesday, and then to yoga on Wednesday." She is an inspiration to us all.

Enid has had a fair amount of recognition. In 2012, she shared an induction to the ICC Hall of Fame with Brian Lara in Colombo. Rachael Heyhoe Flint and Belinda Clark were the only other female occupants at the time. She was named one of *Wisden*'s greatest ever female cricketers in 2014, and in 2015 she received the Lifetime Achievement Award at the *Sunday Times* and Sky Sports Sportswomen of the Year Awards. These are not insignificant awards, but Enid, although delighted by them, seems also bemused, with a lovely mixture of modesty and down-to-earthness. In 2019, Enid received an MBE in the New Year's Honours. This award has a satisfying hint of symmetry about it as Enid explains, "When we beat the Australian team in 1973, Princess Anne came to award the winning trophy to Rachael. And she was in charge when I went to Buckingham Palace to collect my MBE with my three children."

She moved back to her roots in 2011, when Lynne was expecting her first child. Colin became unwell, so she moved back into his bungalow to care for him. "He died aged 86," she tells me, "which was the same as his highest score at cricket. I found him on the floor dead, and so I can't sleep in that room. Instead, I sleep in the single bedroom next to the toilet." This weaving of humour into the solemn fabric of life and death is a habit of hers. It is a character trait of a remarkable person, one who has dealt with life's trials with pragmatism, humour and courage. There are no histrionics, no dramas, but a steady realism. To remain a woman cricketer in the era during which she played for England must have required that 'get on with it' wartime spirit.

When I ask Enid about her most important achievements, she says, "I helped to show cricket wasn't just a man's game. Rachael took us all over England to let us play against men so that people would know that WOMEN DID PLAY CRICKET." And that's it exactly. Enid didn't play the ukulele outside of Lord's to advertise that women were playing cricket as Rachael did, nor did she endlessly fund-raise, but she used her ability on the pitch to prove her point. Today, she unreservedly supports women's cricket, at which she is regular attender. And when she's not keeping fit, she's a big campaigner for the Labour Party, fighting for the workers of the world.

Bharat Sundaresan

HE'S NOT HARD TO SPOT. There aren't too many long-haired, bead-wearing, loud-clothed cricket journalists. Turn on your television and follow an Australian cricket series, he'll be there, personality pulsating through him as he fidgets facts and opinions with contagious energy. His joie de vivre is palpable. The life and soul of any party. A man who works ferociously, with one-eyed focus, and possesses a cricket memory that is close to photographic.

Throughout his life he's been the odd one out, the one that your mother wouldn't approve of, the deliberately defiant one who hasn't bowed to convention. I'd say he was a sheep in wolf's clothing, if a sheep didn't imply following others. Despite a youth scarred by the social infection of substance abuse, and despite his unconventional new-age appearance, he's become one of the most popular cricket journalists in Australia. And cricket, he claims, has saved his life.

When I talk to Bharat Sundaresan via zoom, it is early morning for him, barking dogs as the backdrop to his sunny Adelaide home; late at night in the dark and the drizzle for me. Knowing his rock 'n' roll history, I have already started to write up his psychological casebook in my head, believing him to be the possessor of an addictive personality. During our discussion though, my internal jury wavers, the verdict becomes blurred. Is it possible to have an addictive personality? I'm not so sure. More likely perhaps that some disparate traits and a whole heap of experiences can lead different people to become addicted to a variety of things, depending on other factors. Modern society is all too quick to put us into boxes, and sometimes people can't be boxed. It is Bharat's uniqueness that makes him who he is. And it was circumstances, not just predisposed attributes, that saw him follow a well-trodden path to drug-abuse; a path that he needed to re-route. And cricket, mixed with his natural ability to retain and relate information, provided the necessary direction.

Bharat now holds the impressive position of Australian correspondent and senior writer for Cricbuzz in Australia and is a regular commentator for SEN radio. He has written several books about cricket, and absolutely anyone I ask about him – and I have asked quite a few – say he's 'a ripper'. But his early life was not the obvious starting point for such a prodigious career. He grew up in a teetotal South Indian household. His parents moved from their ancestral roots down south in Chennai over 1,000 miles up to Mumbai. "My family was very conservative – no meat, no eggs, no alcohol. I wouldn't say we were very religious, but my parents were pretty pious," says Bharat. He attributes this piety to a lack of awareness and an ignorance of other people's lives, a naivety that he feels was widespread at that time. "India started opening up in the 1990s, right when I was growing up. I was born in 1985, and by 1991 globalisation had become a thing in India. Access to American television was a great escape into this foreign world." The conventions that the generation above him had followed without question were being challenged by new global influences, and Bharat, like many of his peers, found those influences extremely appealing.

His relationship with his conventional parents was one thing, his relationship with his brother Sid, six years his senior, quite another. It was Sid's treatment of him, Bharat explains, that led to "crazy insecurities". His brother, he tells me, was raised by their grandmother, who spoiled him and brought him up in a very different fashion to other children. As a result, when she died he wasn't aware of how to relate to others or how to treat a younger brother. "I was an easy-going child," he explains, "and I was friendly with everyone. But I don't think it was my popularity that he punished me for, I just think he didn't know how to behave. He would regularly beat me and sometimes hold my head and smash it against the wall. It was so difficult being at home because I had to think twice before saying anything, even if it was a good-mood day for him. I didn't know what my identity was because I had to play this double life. I was this popular child outside, but an extremely cautious one indoors."

A tale of bullying wasn't something I had anticipated. Bharat is so open and so honest as he talks about his childhood, his easy manner suggesting that he's shared the story of this brutality many times before. The detached calmness makes it feel as though he's referring to someone else. That self-control, the caution he talks about, is long gone. The Bharat I am talking to is the popular child, the extrovert, the one with a self-assured freedom that comes with security. Bharat is totally charming. How terribly frustrating for an older brother that must have been, how much he must have wanted to beat it out of him. The most puzzling thing, I suggest to him, is how this bullying seems to have gone unnoticed by his parents. It's a question he gets asked a lot. He says, "My father was away working and was rarely home. On Sundays, I would beg my father to stay, but he never could, and my mother was too timid to stand up for me when he wasn't there. When I went to my father expecting protection, he would say, 'Oh, I've been a younger brother all my life, we all get beaten up.' And historically, whenever I would tell people about my brother, they would say the usual, 'Oh, yeah, man, brothers, right!!' And I'm like, no, no, no, this is beyond that, it's weird, it's serious."

It went unchecked, and if it wasn't for the brothers' joint love of cricket, which cemented their relationship by way of 22 yards of concrete, most of his home-life would have been a waking nightmare. Bharat credits Sid with instilling in him a deep love of the game, and it was this love of cricket, he claims, that kept him sane. If they were watching together, he would be fine. In fact, if they stuck to cricket in any context then they could relate to each other on an equal level. Not only would they play it endlessly, but they would talk about it, not just in passing but in depth, and Bharat became a skilled negotiator, aware that cricket could be the balm that kept him safe. "I learned a lot because of my brother. He would always tell me that we should sit and listen to the commentary. Most people, especially in the sub-continent, just liked watching cricket in a group, which meant they constantly chatted. Nobody would listen, so nobody would know who was who. We knew about more obscure people, like Robin Jackman and Trevor Quirk. We knew Richie Benaud and Bill Lawry. I always give people the example of knowing, as a six-year-old, how many fifties Geoff Marsh scored in the '92 World Cup." "Go on," I ask, "how many?"

Bharat was the go-to cricket guru. "I really don't know how," he claims modestly, but he felt that maybe it was because he paid attention, and because the action on the pitch wasn't always the main attraction for him. "I was always more intrigued by the back story, of who's who, where they come from." He would devour the *Sports Star* magazine, never imagining that he would later become a journalist. This was pre-internet, so his encyclopaedic knowledge was unusual, and all the more impressive for its novelty.

In the age of Tendulkar and the inevitable idolisation of Indian cricketers, his love of the game took an interesting twist when he was a small child. He didn't support India. It's easy to understand for example why those of us who grew up in the 1970s and '80s love West Indian cricket. It was their overwhelming power and their joy in the game. They visited countries and, because of what happened on the cricket-field, transformed home supporters into West Indian supporters. But Bharat wasn't party to that adulation. He was born in 1985, the Windies' best days nearly behind them, and in India there was a growing swell of fandom for the increasingly successful Indian side. "I was like, 'Oh, so you guys are going to get obsessed with India, I'm going to get obsessed with something else', but there has to be some reason why, as a five-year-old, I started cheering like crazy for the West Indies!"

It's rare at such a young age not to follow the flock. Bharat was already on the journey that saw him donning loud colours and growing that threatening hair. He jokes with me that he would have been burnt alive if people knew he celebrated the fall of Sachin Tendulkar's wicket. "My parents would have been, 'Well, yeah, he deserved it!'" But I think this is key. It's so much easier to be part of a group. Bharat didn't want simply to follow the path of least resistance. On a date etched into his memory – 29 July 2002 –his brother left to work in America. Bharat had finally found what felt like a unique freedom.

At the age of sixteen, he became the vocalist of a heavy metal band and, rather like a prisoner released from incarceration, he began the life of a heavy metal dude with the fervour of someone freed from his shackles. "I was like, 'Wow, this is the life'. I felt like I was finally living and being myself." It started very harmlessly, Bharat tells me. He did a few gigs, had a puff of a spliff afterwards. But it moved on quite rapidly, there were older kids, some of them from college, who liked his singing and invited him to parties. "I'm sixteen years old," he says, "and there were these eighteen-year-old girls praising my vocals and so, at that point, whether they ask you to smoke or whatever they ask, you're doing it." Before he knew it, he was part of a drug culture; he'd found his rebellion. "I wasn't surprised that I was drawn into anything. When I look back at it, I think I was doing it because of peer pressure, and wanting to be the guy who has a better capacity than everyone else as well. I could drink more, I could smoke more."

This rock 'n' roll lifestyle was intoxicating, and it allowed him to draw away from his home life. "I wasn't there, I wasn't on this planet," he says, and he fell further and further into a drug-hazed oblivion, hardly going home. His darkest phase, he feels, was when he was going to bed at six in the morning after a whole night of partying and then was up by eleven to go to the local Indian bar called Noon, where all the stock traders would go after their lunch. "It was basically open for the middle-aged Gujarati men, but we'd be there, four or five of us, just drinking our days away."

In hindsight, it's easy to see that a suppressed childhood had naturally led to this extreme escapism. But Bharat wasn't an addict in the true sense of the word. "I was a people-pleaser," he explains. There came a point, eventually, when he wasn't enjoying himself. He would sit in the bar and wonder what he was doing, questioning what kind of life it was. "But I would still do it," he laughs. "I did a lot of things which I didn't necessarily enjoy, and I'd do them because I thought that's what I was supposed to do." He was the entertainer, the life of the party, "and I hadn't realised just how much it had taken over my life". He smiles. He smiles a lot. It shows how affable he is and how readily he puts people at ease. It's not hard to see how he became an important part of this heavy metal group.

Bharat moved from vocals to drums, and he was always there, the one with the car. The getaway driver. "Around 2006," he laughs, "I realised that we kept saying we were a heavy metal band, but we never seemed to practise much. We just got together to get high and dream of all the gigs that we could be playing. This frustration led to the first time I overdosed." Bharat, with a knowing nod, admits it was a scary experience. He'd seen other people overdosing and being rushed to hospital, "but I'd built up an invincibility complex, which meant that I always thought I could hold my drugs better than anyone else." He's analysed it many times, I can tell, and we discuss for a while how death feels so far away from the young. Instead of this dangerous experience making him more vulnerable, he somehow came to feel even more invincible. Not just that, but cooler, more interesting, the dude of dudes. "People were like, 'Oh, you know what happened to Bharat and he got over it. He survived. He's cool.' And because I had one of those experiences where I remembered everything, I became like Martin Scorsese. I had my own cult movie, and people would sit around and ask me to tell them about what happened. They were like, 'Oh, dude, tell me again, man, that's so trippy. Let's do more drugs.' They were tripping on my overdose story." It was Bharat through the looking-glass.

Bharat was unsettled. On the one hand, he understood the significance of an overdose, but on the other it was hard not to bask in the glory of the cult status it brought him. At the same time, his parents had noticed that he wasn't doing anything constructive with his life, that something was not right with him. "I never looked drunk in front of them or misbehaved," he explains. As far as his parents were concerned, being 'drunk' meant being found unconscious at the side of the road. They knew he had a car and that he'd had no accidents, and they knew that he hung around with other long-haired people, but nobody had got killed. Drugs had no place in their world. They called on his brother and, as usual, his solution was to fix him. This 'fixing' was a beating. But these brotherly tactics didn't work, Bharat wasn't a small child any longer. Bullying wasn't on the cards for an older, surer-of-himself young band member. When his father suggested that he should either join his business or go to America, like his brother, Bharat realised that he needed to do something. It was 2007, and he was 21. He needed to find a direction. "That's when the whole journalism course got discussed. Someone said your son is obsessed with cricket, he should try writing because he tells stories all the time." And it was true, Bharat admits, he even made a story out of his overdose. He knew that, so far in his life, he'd done nothing to please his parents, and so he agreed to apply. "I remember going for this interview for the course run by a Hindu paper in Chennai. I could see everyone else dressed formally, and I'm dressed like I just walked down from the Himalayas somewhere. That was the only time I remember feeling sort of out of place, and hearing parents whispering to their daughters to stay away from that boy, he's got long hair."

Much to his surprise, Bharat was offered a place on the course, and suddenly there was only a month before he had to leave for Chennai. "It was a big deal for a lot of my friends because not only was I the life and soul, but I was also the driver who got them home." As a result, the leaving party was huge, and it was there, deliberately partying harder than everyone else, that he overdosed for the second time. This time he didn't feel in control. "First time it was a new experience. This time I was sinking, and as I could feel myself slipping, I was saying to myself, 'if I don't fight this now, I will die a loser. I cannot die a loser.'" It's a line, he claims, that has become the motto of his life. He remembers vividly thinking that he couldn't die ashamed. "I almost gave up. It's like when you're sinking in water, which almost happened to me once, when I was trying to teach this guy how to swim. I knew how to swim. He didn't. I got a little brave, and as soon as he lost his footing, he climbed on me. And then he started pushing me down as he held on to me. Again, that was a near-death experience, where I was yelling out stuff and swallowing a lot of water as well as inhaling it. And then, after a while, I remember feeling so powerless, I couldn't do anything. My arms weren't moving. And I thought, 'I'm dead.' So that's what it felt like, the second overdose, and I could feel my heart just getting weaker and weaker."

Bharat's strength of character, and a desperate need not to let people down, saw him survive. It was a grand finale to a phase of his life that had provided an escape from his family, and had confirmed that, yes, he was popular. Yes, he was the life and soul. And yes, he was better, way better, than his brother ever allowed him to be. But such a drug-dependent life was never going to lead to success. Bharat had a whole lot more to offer. He had been lucky not to be hospitalised, lucky to survive, and now he had an opportunity to enter the next chapter of his life, a chapter that would rescue him and ultimately lead on to greater things. We ponder for a while over whether, if it hadn't been for the fact that he had sunk so low, he would ever have been in a position to consider cricket as a career? It's an interesting question but, as often with interesting questions, there is no simple answer. What's clear, though, is that Bharat could now begin to shape the career that he was always meant to have.

He needed a break from Mumbai, a break from his heavy metal lifestyle. He went to distant Chennai to begin his ten-month course at the Asian College of Journalism, with no other immediate thoughts than to be away from Mumbai. He joined 110 other wannabe journalists, with no idea what he was getting into, or why it was there that he had ended up. "None of the Faculty gave me a chance. They were like, 'This guy has just come from nowhere.' I remember them saying to my face, 'Look, you spend your ten months here, have a good time, and then go back to wherever you came from. We're focused on all these other kids, because they're journalists. We can recognise a journalist when we see one.'"

And, for a while, Bharat fell into the role of the party animal again, this time with alcohol. Since his second overdose, he has never touched drugs. At 22, he was a similar age to many of the students, but most came from smaller Indian cities, towns and villages. For them, to come to Chennai was the start of their liberation. They began smoking and drinking. Unlike them, "I almost felt like a retired Test cricketer going to play Under-19 World Cups. It was like I'd been in this movie before. Having said that, because of the way I looked, it was easy for me to score weed for them. They would come to me and I would help them roll a joint and give it to them."

This makes me smile. I can't help but think this is like the driver role. Bharat making himself indispensable again, an enabler. It's the people-pleaser in him, and it's a definite character trait, one that remains with him, although I suspect that he's more circumspect in his pleasing. He had stopped taking drugs, but he was drinking a lot to stay sociable. The course, he tells me, was unsatisfying, but it did get him into the habit of writing. "I could always write," he explains, "all my school essays were on cricket, but I didn't do it on a daily basis. The course moulded my ability, and I started enjoying the writing aspect more than anything else."

He tells me of a time on the course that he feels sums up the general vibe. "We watched a black-and-white movie, and then had a discussion about it, I thought I might learn something and maybe have something to add, but then one guy got up and said, 'I love the way they use the reds and blues', and everyone started nodding. And I'm like, 'What are they talking about? Where did they see reds and blues, it's a black-and-white movie. What am I doing with my life? Maybe I should start doing drugs again?'"

Bharat was the one everyone wanted to party with, but as far as the course was concerned, he only really knew about sport. He wanted to prove to the others that he could do other things and so, for his dissertation, he went to a tutor with a proposal to write about the occult. "She was literally rolling on the floor laughing, so I felt a little hurt. But she said something that made sense. She told me my strength was in cricket, so do something on cricket." He ended up writing about Tendulkar, and it seems that Bharat's writing, like his speaking, was fast. It took him hours, not days. He later emulated this speed-writing with his books which, he claims, have taken only a few days to write. "You can go off people," I tell him.

Despite his antipathy towards the course, it led to two things that were instrumental in helping to change his life. The first was meeting, while on it, his future wife, Isha Chatterjee. The second was the opening it provided for an interview at a big newspaper. "Meeting Isha," Bharat admits, "was more significant than anything else that happened during those ten months." He had walked into a lab to use a computer, and, seeing her sitting in a corner, with 50 other students watching, he – the long-haired one draped in beads – walked straight up to her and told her she was the most beautiful girl he'd ever seen. The room went quiet as she silently thanked him. Bharat puts this down to his lack of filters, and yes, to some extent that's true. He definitely lacks the filters of conventionality that lead us to conform, but it's also his raw honesty. He says he wasn't trying to hit on her, he just thought she should know. Unorthodox it might have been, but it kick-started a friendship. They were both misfits, he explains, neither desperate to be journalists. Isha was there at her father's behest, Bharat there because he had to be somewhere. Neither saw red and blue in a black-and-white movie, neither followed the student fashion of endlessly quoting Noam Chomsky.

It was just before he was due to attend the interview at *Indian Express* that Bharat, a man who likes to teeter on the edge of self-destruction, nearly made a decision that could have seen him lose his footing. "I remember so vividly the day I had my interview with the paper that I eventually joined for over 10 years", and he recalls an obviously well-rehearsed tale. "Megadeth was playing in Bangalore, and all my friends from Chennai were pleading with me, saying, 'Fuck it, mate, what do you mean interview? This is Megadeth! Megadeth has come to India for the first time. We play Megadeth. We have to see them.' I almost went. I had a train ticket booked the previous night, but something made me stay and go for this one job interview." We talk for a while about the sliding-doors scenario of what if? It has many layers to it and, for some reason, Bharat's choices seem more precarious than most other people's. Would he have fallen back into his Mumbai ways? I can almost visualise the devil and the angel above each shoulder egging him on. "I know I would have seen Megadeath live," he offers, "but I got to see them at another time anyway. Again, all these things, it was like happenstance. All my decisions in life have been taken on the split-second, and this one completely changed my life." And it did.

Bharat got the *Indian Express* job at the interview. It took him back up to Mumbai. "It was the perfect paper for me," he says. It gave him the freedom and the boss he needed. "He could be nasty," Bharat says, "but he brought out the best in me." The first couple of months meant his nights would end at 2 or even 3 am, a time that he was quite used to and one, as he admits, that kept him away from his friends, but it wasn't too long before he struck gold and covered his first Ranji Trophy match. He had an extremely lucky break when one of the paper's cricket writers left at just the right time.

I realise, at this point, that Bharat is not only the fastest talker I have ever interviewed, but also the one who could most easily chat his way out of, or indeed into, nearly anything. With a gap in the cricket section of the paper, his boss took a punt on him, and he was asked to cover an international game: India v England. He was right where he wanted to be.

"This was within five months of me becoming a journalist, which was unheard of at the time, especially for a kid with long hair working for a national daily. It was 2008. To become a successful journalist you had to go through the grind and climb each step one at a time." Bharat took a flying leap to the top, and he didn't look back. His first big story was a controversy at the newly formed Indian Premier League. It was the only time the IPL had African-origin cheerleaders, and they'd been racially abused. "My editor sent me to the press conference they were appearing in with their handler, and when I came back I sat down on a chair with my teeny-tiny shorts, and he asks me what happened and where were my notes? I looked at him and asked, 'Notes?' I just showed him my hand and said, 'These are the names of the two women, everything else is up there,' and I pointed to my head. And he's like, 'No, that's not how you do journalism. You need notes,' and he just shook his head and walked away."

Bharat wrote the story and, inevitably, they all loved it. As he explains, "I became an urban legend in my office!" His colleagues would come to him and ask, 'How do you remember all of this?' And he told them that was how he'd always done it. A defiance maybe? A nod to the unconventional definitely, but this was Bharat. "I've always done things my own way. Not because I want to stand out, but that's the only way I know to do things." And I can't help admitting that it's fair enough. Why should there be one specific way to do something?

Bharat was starting to make inroads into the world of journalism, and he was following the game he knew and loved so well. He may well have looked different, but people were starting to concede that he might have long hair, but have you read what he writes? The writing was superseding the anti-establishment image. What he wrote started to matter more than what he looked like.

Bharat worked for the *Indian Express* as special correspondent/ cricket writer for over ten years, and then in 2018, Isha was offered a job in Australia. "I contacted CricBuzz, who I knew had always wanted me to work for them, and told them I was moving to live there." His contact suggested that he apply to be CricBuzz's Australian correspondent and a senior mentor. "Fair enough," I say (I guess they had suggested this to him in the past), "but isn't this asking for your perfect job and moulding it around your life?" I laugh in admiration. Bharat was in such demand that he could choose his dream role. He continued to write prolifically, including the best-selling book *The Dhoni Touch* in 2018 and *Believe* with Suresh Raina in 2021. In 2023 he co-authored *The Miracle Makers*, about the Indian 2020 tour of Australia. He also took up commentary for SEN, a Melbourne-based radio station and is now a well-known voice. Never one to shy away from tackling important topics, in 2022 he published an article in the Australian daily newspaper *The Age*, where he told Australia to end racism, revealing in his article that even after five years his accreditation was often questioned on entry to a ground.

He and Isha were happily ensconced in Adelaide, his favourite Australian city. "It was like a lot of things in my life, it just kind of sort of fell into place … The first time I visited Australia I fell in love with the country, and especially Adelaide. I mean Sydney and Melbourne are great cities, but you know, just something about

Adelaide charmed me the first time I came here. It was quaint, but at the same time it still had a bit of a feel of a city. So it just kind of worked out well. But then Australia has given me so much." In 2023, he dedicated *The Miracle Makers* to Australia, 'for accepting all of me, especially the cornucopia of colours, the chatter and the hair.' "Australia," he tells me, "told me, hey, you know what? There's nothing wrong with you, just be yourself. It has meant a lot to me. I felt like a pariah, and I was always looking for a place which would accept me. This is the place which tells me you do what you want to do. We'll be amused at times. We will laugh at you, but you don't have to change. That's fine, nobody's going to judge you."

Australia obviously has made a huge impression on Bharat, and I venture to ask him whether that is how he feels about cricket? "Oh, more than anything else, like I mean I credit Australia a lot for what's happened, but cricket! I've always said I owe my life to cricket. Like, you know, if not for cricket, I would have died. I would have done a lot more of what I was doing back then if I didn't have that sobering thing of cricket. I had to be the guy, the cricket guy. And it was just like predestined."

David Lloyd

IN 1989, THERE WAS A MEMORABLE TV ADVERT, made by the Milk Marketing Board and featuring a Scouse lad drinking copious amounts of milk from the fridge. He quotes the claim of the great Liverpool striker, Ian Rush, that he would only have been good enough to play for Accrington Stanley if he hadn't drunk his milk. His friend disparagingly asks, 'Accrington Stanley, who are they?' and the lad, with milk-stained mouth, replies, 'Exactly!' The advert, like David Lloyd before it, made Accrington, with or without Stanley, a household name.

David, or Bumble as he is affectionately known, due to his apparent similarity to the Bumblies (Michael Bentine's creations for children's TV), is a true cricketing all-rounder. He has not only played for his country but also coached them and commentated on them. In addition, he has captained his county, Lancashire, and umpired professionally. His name is synonymous with cricket, but this larger-than-life character sprang from very humble beginnings in the once-prosperous textile town of Accrington, and it's plain to see that he couldn't be prouder of his Lancashire heritage.

I have met David a few times now. Without fail, he has a wide smile on his face and a glint in his eye. This time we have to resort to Zoom. It's not the same, but it doesn't seem to stem his Lancashire-lilting liveliness, nor curb his gift of the gab. "OK, rock on," he nods at me. I want to know about his childhood, so we start there. "I had a very modest family background. My house was a two-up, two-down with an outside toilet. My dad was a lay preacher, and he ran the local football team."

That team was Cedar Swifts FC, later Cambridge Street Methodists. Football, David explains, was responsible for his getting involved in cricket at an early age. "The goalkeeper for the local football team was called Peter Westwell, and he was involved at Accrington Cricket Club. I always went along with Dad to all the football – come hail, rain or shine – so Peter got to know me. He paid my subscription for junior membership at Accrington, so I would go up there on my bicycle, and we had nets for juniors and nets for seniors. I would probably be about ten at that time."

David also played cricket at his local primary school, although, as he explains, they weren't blessed with public-school facilities.

"There was no yard or field or anything. We just had an enthusiastic teacher, Mr. Wade. We would have about four matches against other local schools on any sort of area that we could find. The other boys were two or three years older than me. I was playing when I was about nine, they were closer to twelve." "Did you play with a hard ball?" I ask him, fascinated to hear that there used to be cricket in primary schools. "Yeah," he answers, "it was a compound ball, and there was a local playing field which was about half a mile away. We'd have to go in twos across the main road, with Mr. Wade watching, and we'd get some sort of game going in a lesson, which should last about half an hour. And then we had to come back about half a mile." Health and safety would have a field day today. "It was the same for football as well." It's then that he adds, "I was quite an outstanding young footballer." Nothing boastful or arrogant and no false modesty. David Lloyd says it like it is.

"Tell me about your parents," I say. A lot is known about David's career, but not much about his childhood. His evocative and characterful descriptions don't disappoint. I've never been an avid viewer of Coronation Street, but it feels to me that David's parents wouldn't have looked out of place in Weatherfield. "My Dad was unbelievably quiet," he tells me. This surprises me, and I look at him slightly incredulously, asking the inevitable "Where did you get it from then?" "My mother was one of thirteen," he replies, a huge smile on his always expressive face, "so she had to stand up to be heard. She was a firebrand, was my mother. And I've got that trait. You know, she wouldn't stand any nonsense from anybody. Whereas my dad just used to do his work, come home and give my mum his wage packet. My mum would give him 10 shillings out of it, then she'd put little bits of money in a box for the electricity and in another box for the gas. It all went into little boxes." This feels like looking through a leaded window into a bygone era.

"What did your dad do?" I ask. "Initially, he worked in a foundry, which was proper hard work, but his main working life was at the hospital, finishing up as the operating theatre technician. He would prepare the theatre for operations and then clean up after and make sure everything was sterilised. And me being just a young kid, I didn't know the difference between theatre and cinema, and I thought he worked at the pictures."

"And did you have siblings?" I ask. "No, I'm the only one. They were thirty-seven when they had me. My mother never tired of telling me that she wanted a girl, and they were going to call this girl Gwyneth, because there's a Welsh connection within the family. So she dressed me as Gwyneth for a number of years, and I never had my hair cut. I had the longest tresses you could imagine, and she used to put my hair in curlers, so that it had a wave, and I'd look absolutely like Marilyn Monroe." This makes me laugh a lot. There aren't many people who look less like Marilyn Monroe, and the image of a young David with flowing blonde hair standing over a subway grate is an amusing one. "It was only when I started kicking people around at football that they decided they'd better let me carry on as a lad. As I told you, I was outstanding at football and I'd take no prisoners, never mind my streaming curls." A few years later, in the late 1960s and early 1970s, I suggest, his hairstyle would have fitted in perfectly.

David was regularly playing football as well as cricket and was good enough to play semi-professionally for Accrington Stanley. It was far from inevitable that he would choose to make his career in cricket. "So why did you go for cricket rather than football?" I ask. "Because I was deemed too small for football and, as I got older and started playing serious cricket, I discovered that I was good at it. And I got more timid at football. I wouldn't go into tackles. I wouldn't do the dirty work." But there was another reason as well. David admits that the quality of the players at Accrington CC was a real pull. "We had stellar professionals at Accrington, including Bobby Simpson, Wes Hall and Eddie Barlow." The Lancashire Leagues were littered with real giants of the game, and these three world-class players were compelling presences. "I was about 13, and playing in the twos, when Wes Hall took a real shine to me and really encouraged me. He got me bowling wrist spinners out of the back of my hand. I was a bit of an unusual left-arm spinner, and the seniors would invite me from time to time to bowl at them. Then I got picked in the first team." "You must have been pretty young to play in the first team," I say. "Yeah, I would have been fourteen. I got three wickets in my first game, and they were really good league players."

When he started at senior school, Accrington Secondary Technical School, one of his teachers, Mr. Cunliffe, said that he'd heard about

David's cricket and sent him for Lancashire schoolboy trials. "This was played on the square at Old Trafford and all," he tells me, raising those trademark pointy eyebrows. "You're absolutely in the market-place playing at the ground. There was a committee of twelve businessmen there watching you. I got runs and wickets for North Lancashire against South Lancashire, and I obviously impressed because, as soon as I left school, they signed me up immediately."

At sixteen, David found himself not only playing cricket for his county but also provided with a winter occupation. "They signed me on an apprenticeship, which meant that during the winter I worked on the ground. They had their own maintenance staff, including plumbers, electricians and joiners. So, during the winter months, I was seconded to the joinery team." This smacks of simpler times, when 'professional sportsman' was a job, not a way to reach mega-stardom and millionaire status. There's a touch of old-style National Service about it. It could be argued that an apprenticeship provided players not only with the money to see them through the winter months, but also an auxiliary skill for their post-cricket careers. Not that they had much choice about it. David explains, "It was unheard of to say 'I'm going to South Africa or I'm going to Australia' during the winter. That just wasn't on the agenda. In our area you would play football at the weekends in the winter, and cricket in summer. Weekdays in the winter, you'd get on with your work."

For David, both work and cricket meant a six o'clock bus from home (with his kit in the summer), then transferring to another bus to take him through Manchester to Old Trafford. "I was given permission to get there at half past eight instead of eight because there were no available buses. It was the same for cricket and for the winter." I question David as to whether he ever had time to stop and think whether he actually wanted to play cricket for a living. "I knew through playing in the Lancashire Leagues, which I played in for two years, that I wanted to play cricket." There's not a hint of doubt in his answer. "I had a fierce determination. And it's funny, I've got lifelong friendships from that time, because other lads who were in that league team would go on to be county cricketers as well."

"Were your parents really pleased that you went into cricket, or did they just accept it?" I ask, wanting to find out if they understood the significance of playing for your county for a living. "Yeah, they just accepted it. My dad always gave me quiet encouragement. Nothing from my mum, but she had several brothers, and my uncles were all like second dads, and they were supportive. Everybody knew them in Accrington. 'Don't mess with the Aspins. Don't upset the Aspins.' That's my mother's side. My Dad was totally the opposite. He was such a gentle soul. He would go to church three times a day, and he would go out and preach anywhere that would have him."

There's a real tenderness when he talks about his father, and a baffled amusement when he mentions what he was like in his later years. "When he was in his nineties, he was still going out. I just looked at him and thought he's got half his breakfast down his front and he's going around in a pair of old tracksuit bottoms." "So, he lived until he was in his nineties. What about your mum?" I ask. "My mum died in her late seventies. She had cancer of the spine, and she went pretty quickly." I may be wrong, but I can't imagine that his dad's breakfast would have been splattered down his front when she was around. His uncles, David tells me, did not have long lives. "I grew up in an era when everybody smoked. All my uncles, and my cousins. I have that many cousins. I've got cousins who I don't know are my cousins, and cousins born out of wedlock, who have different names, but they're my cousins. Anyway, they all smoked. I remember all their fingers looked like they were burnt because they were so brown with nicotine, because they were smoking the strongest cigarettes you could imagine, Capstan or Senior Service, Craven A or Woodbines. They all died young. I have one notable uncle – Uncle Larry – who lasted till he were about forty-two, and he used to chew Condor tobacco. It was a good effort to reach forty-two, really." David goes on to explain that, as a child, he was asthmatic, so he didn't smoke and found it hard to be around so much smoking. The asthma left him when he was about twenty-one. You could argue that asthma helped him avoid the fate of his uncles.

Interested to understand whether his move into county cricket was a lucrative one, I ask David whether the wage of a cricketer/joiner was a good one. "It were less than normal," he laughs. "They gave me £7 a week. I had to go to the office, and I'd get a little brown envelope with £7 in it. I went home, gave it to my mum and she gave me a pound back." Surprised, I say, "So she did the same with your wages as she did with your dad's?" "Yep, it all went into the little boxes." Seven pounds a week doesn't sound a whole lot of money, but David went on to explain that "when I joined officially with a contract, it went down to £6 a week but, you know, that was still more than what my dad were getting." This emphasises his 'modest upbringing'. I remind myself that it's all relative. Perhaps it wasn't so little after all! "Was it the same wage when you were a joiner in the winter?" "Yes, £6 across the board."

It wasn't easy or straightforward to get your own living arrangements in this era, so David lived at home for the first few years of his time with Lancashire. His wages carried on disappearing into his mother's boxes: boxes that were essential to the maintenance of a small household. When I ask him how long he stayed living at home, David is quick to point out that there were societal rules that people like him were expected to follow. These included assumptions about the 'right time' to settle down with someone in your own home. "It was an unwritten law that you didn't get married until you were twenty-one, and any sort of sexual activity was also out of the window until then." David kept his side of the 'law', but only just. "I was twenty-one in March and, for tax reasons, you had to get married by the end of March. So we got married just as I turned twenty-one in 1968."

He did, however, defy his mother, and had to deal with her wrath for some time afterwards, when he climbed onto the property ladder. "My wife and I, who are now divorced, bought a house. We got a mortgage, and my mother wouldn't speak to me, because that meant owing money. You don't owe money! It took me mum a long time to come to terms with the fact that we'd got this little semi-detached dormer bungalow, and we owed money on it." It's hard to imagine in our credit-happy society just how frowned upon it was to be in debt, but David was keen enough to start his married life in his own place to risk upsetting the ruler of his roost. And he clearly felt settled enough in his work to burden himself with a mortgage.

David's career was taking off. He started at Lancashire as a left-arm spinner batting at around number eight. "Gradually," he tells me, "the batting developed, and then quite quickly I was starting to excel at it." He made his first-class debut in 1965, when his first match at Old Trafford, against Middlesex, saw him get an ignominious pair. He struggled in his first season, certainly with the bat. In his thirteen matches, he amassed only 262 runs at a dismal average of 14.55. He was more successful with his bowling, bagging 21 wickets at a reasonable 31.33. 1966 was a better year for the Championship, but he struggled with the one-day game. It was not until 1968 that he scored his first century for Lancashire, against Cambridge University. Wikipedia records that he told the *Sunday Times* that this was the moment he realised he wanted to be a cricketer. No doubt it helped, but David was already feeling at home at Lancashire amongst the stars of the day. "We had good mentors and good senior players around us who would keep you in check or give you encouragement. They would stamp on you if you stepped out of line and very quickly bring you back into line." It sounds like a tough-love environment, but one that David didn't feel out of his depth in. "We had loads of nets," he continues, "and they were so encouraging, you know, giving you little tips and advice."

There are a few times in our conversation when I realise quite how long-reaching David's experiences in the cricketing world span. There was still a strong residue of the old Gentlemen/Players hierarchy. To survive in cricket, deference was helpful. And there was not yet the huge focus on diet, exercise, well-being and 'health and safety'. Certainly, the legislation was not as strict, with the guidelines more blurred. David explains that, remarkably, during his time at the club, the Lancashire coach was head-hunted from Worcestershire at the ripe old age of seventy. "He were a chap called Charles Hallows, who played for Lancashire in the 1930s, one of the very few players to get 1,000 runs before the end of May. He was really good to me, and the tales he told us all about the dressing-room in the 1930s were absolutely hilarious. He said, for example, that when we played at Taunton, who weren't very good in them days, if we won the toss and batted, the first five would stay at the ground and the rest of us would go to the pictures." It feels a bit like the plot of a *Carry On* film, with Sid James leading them into trouble, and the unlucky Kenneth Connor being the cricketer to cop the flak, the one with the incriminating evidence of cinema ticket-stubs planted on him. David explains that Charles said that, in those days, there was always a crate of beer in the changing-room, highlighting the stark difference of today's energy drinks and hydration breaks.

Keen to see if this legacy continued into David's playing days, I ask him what it was like to be part of the Lancashire dressing-room. I want to know the inside story, but he's not forthcoming with details. "Throughout my career it was always a fabulous dressing-room, but I'm a great believer in 'what happens in there stays in there'. It's my place and I'm not sharing the details. It can be cruel. It can be hilarious. It can be uplifting. It can be dangerous. But as soon as you step out of it, it's gone. I had one player who got hold of me by the throat and shoved me up against the wall, and I was captain at the time. But when we left the changing-room, we went and had a beer."

I ask him if it was a fulfilling career, and his words spill out in a wave of contagious enthusiasm. "You know, every day is a great day. There was a discipline about playing county cricket as it was at that time. There were ups and downs, and you just had to try and stay level. You get out for nought; you play a bad shot, and then another time you get 100. You're playing in a topsy-turvy sort of atmosphere, but your team-mates help you along. I tell you though," he adds, "that the team element goes out of the window when it's you and Andy Roberts or it's you and Imran Khan. You know, he's got a ball, I've got a bat. The team element really only comes into play when you're fielding. And then when you're in the changing-room."

He laughs. "I think that's what makes cricket such a great game," I offer, "that it has both." "Yeah, it is," he replies, and then he's in full flow once more. "And again, we had great encounters. There was Joel Garner at Somerset, Mike Procter at Gloucestershire, Malcolm Marshall at Hampshire. You know, you're playing against the greatest, and for a lad from Accrington to come and compete with these guys, I just kept thinking 'I've come a long way, I'm doing alright.'" And that's my interview summed up in one sentence. Cricket took David from a modest, conventional life to the dizzying heights of stardom, stardom that he managed to maintain through his numerous roles at the top of the game.

"You know we've skipped a little bit," David prompts me. He appears to be running the interview now, I note in amusement. "We missed when I became captain. Before that, we were winning everything under one of the greatest men I've ever met, Jack Bond. He was a modest cricketer but a great leader of men. He could lay it down and just let you know who's in charge. But he was revered within the team. We absolutely loved him. And our stardust, of course, was Farokh Engineer and the brilliant Clive Lloyd, who we sometimes lost for months at a time if the West Indies were playing. We won Sunday Leagues. We won Gillette Cups. And when I took over, we were just over the tip and slightly going the other way." Lancashire had won the Gillette Cup in 1970, 1971 and 1972. David took over the captaincy in 1973. He led Lancashire to another Gillette Cup triumph in 1975 and the captaincy didn't seem to affect his own form. He managed to amass 1,405 first-class runs in his first season, including three centuries. He continued to take wickets as well as seeing an improvement in his one-day form.

But Lancashire weren't quite the force that they had been. "We were always hampered by the weather," he explains, going on to lead me down one of his rabbit-holes. "The other thing that we haven't really discussed is uncovered pitches," he says, and his enthusiasm is palpable. "Uncovered pitches were fabulous, because sometimes they'd be totally unplayable, and other times they'd do absolutely nothing. You never really knew how it was going to play. And sometimes, if you had an opportunity on an uncovered pitch to use a roller, you might just kill whatever there was, or it would bring the water to the surface and the ball would do a bit more. They were great, but it was the right thing to do to change to totally covered, but uncovered pitches certainly helped to develop your technique." "I guess, to a lesser degree, the same could be said for helmets?" I suggest. "Without helmets you just got out of the way. Bowlers were bombarding you with bouncers, but sometimes you'd take it on. I would always try and get out of the way, but occasionally you'd make a false move. I had a depressed cheekbone when I got hit in the face. I also got hit in the teeth and once on the head. Three knocks in nineteen years is not too bad."

We don't mention the ball he got from Jeff Thomson that hit him below the belt and incapacitated him for some time in the 1974/75 Ashes. But I hear he dines out on it still. Following a debut for the England one-day side in September 1973, when England lost easily to the West Indies (David making only 8 before being run out), he was a surprise pick for the Test team against India at Lord's in

June 1974. "I only got in the side because Geoffrey Boycott wasn't around, as he reminds me so often," laughs David. It's not hard to imagine the details of this conversation repeated time and again.

"But he was right. I was never going to get in instead of John Edrich, Dennis Amiss or Geoffrey." It was a fortunate injury for one of them. He scored a steady 46 in a Test that saw India lose by an innings. His performance meant he kept his place for the next Test at Edgbaston, where he went on to score an unbeaten 214, with England winning the series 3-0. If he'd never played again for England, he would have ended with a batting average of 260. He didn't fare as well in the Tests against Pakistan which, as he tells me "ended in a bit of acrimony because England were accused of allowing water to get under the pitch deliberately, which would favour Derek Underwood skittling out the opposition." David played in both of the ODIs that followed, hitting 116* from 159 balls at Trent Bridge.

He had impressed enough to keep his place in the England side to tour to Australia in 1974/5. "How was it?" I ask. "It was terrific. I loved every minute of it." And there were a lot of minutes, David tells me. "You know how times have changed. I mean, before the first Test we'd played every state. We must have been away over four months." This epic journey was a much bigger deal in those days. "I'd never been out of the UK, so it was such an adventure to go on an aeroplane, and the journey was around 36 hours." "Did you still have to share rooms then?" I ask him. "Oh God yeah, my first room-mate was Geoff Arnold, then Mike Hendrick. When Colin Cowdrey came out, they put him in with me, but I have to say I never saw him, I don't know where he was." It wasn't a successful tour on the field. David didn't excel, and England were soundly beaten. "They were way better than us. They had a super team. Fantastic captain in Ian Chappell and a great bowling attack led by Lillee and Thomson. They beat us 4-1. A very strong West Indies team followed us, and Australia beat them 5-1."

David came back early from his only England tour with a neck injury. "It's still causing me enormous problems. I've had two recent operations. One of them didn't go as well as expected. And I've been having electric shock treatment on my skull." "How did you injure yourself?" I ask him. "It started with taking evasive action at short leg, and something just went in my neck. It's never really left, and I have these violent headaches which absolutely knock me sideways, but this electric shock treatment seems to be working."

David didn't play for England in Test cricket again, but he had a couple more outings in the one-day side in 1978 and 1980. "I didn't play any more for England until Beefy, in his wisdom, called me back into the side. At the time the counties were playing Benson & Hedges matches, and the West Indies were on tour. We played against Derbyshire and Scotland and I got a hundred in each game, just at the time they were picking the England squad. I thought, 'Christ, I'm going to get picked here', and I was. I think Malcolm Marshall hit me on the arm, and that was the end of that. I should never have played. It was a poor selection."

David continued to play for Lancashire after he stepped down from captaining in 1977, but he found that the neck injury made things difficult at the crease. "I had to adapt my play, and from being stood side-on I stood more square-on, sort of with my shoulders pointing down the pitch, because I couldn't turn sideways. So I was looking straight down, which eliminates the off side unless you're in a full position to square cut. You can't off drive because you haven't enough time to turn your body."

"So it limits you?" I suggest, but no, David replies and with actions too. "No. Well, it didn't because I mean it's a real coaching tactical thing. This is it, a very poor comparison. I'm a left-handed left-hander. Everything I do is left-handed and so the bottom hand is dominant, so everything is going leg side. David Gower is a right-handed left-hander. He's right-handed. He writes right-handed. He would throw right-handed, but he would bat left-handed. His dominant hand is his right, so he's a driver. And, you know, you don't recall David Gower playing big shots over deep mid-wicket. David Gower will ease it through extra cover and backward point again and again." David then, his mind going off on tangents, explains it in golf terms. "David Gower hates golf," he tells me. "He thinks it's the most heathen game that's ever been invented. We were in Johannesburg, and it was raining. The rest of us said, 'Come on, there's a fantastic hangar that sells golf clubs, and you can hit balls for ever indoors.' Gower came with us and picked a club up left-handed and he just fresh-aired. He then picked up a right-handed club and hit them sweet as anything."

"What came next after playing for England. Umpiring or coaching?" I ask. "Umpiring," he tells me. There's such a sharpness to his mind that there isn't a detail he's unsure of, or a part of his life over which his memory seems to falter. "Whilst I was playing and had nothing to do in winter, I took my coaching badges." "So you'd stopped doing your joinery at the ground by then?" "Oh yeah, that was long gone. You know, I chuckle when people say players are fitter these days than we were. Well, in my off-peak time, during the winter, I was loading beer wagons or changing tyres in an outdoor tyre-bay, and you had to be fit to do that."

David did his coaching courses at Lilleshall Sports Centre in Staffordshire while he was still a player. "Did you do umpire courses as well?" I ask. David was shrewd enough to keep one eye on his future. "No, I was a reserve umpire, which meant that I couldn't officiate County Championship matches. I would do Second XI games and university matches. I did all my training in university cricket, standing with an experienced umpire until I became proficient enough to go onto the list, which I did." "Did you enjoy umpiring?" I ask. By now I was anticipating his answers, because I was getting used to his enthusiasm. It's delightful and contagious. "I absolutely loved it. There was never a false word ever. The players were fantastic, because they would know me anyway, and so there was a good rapport. Never had a bad word ever anywhere." There was a points system, he tells me. Umpires were rated on a scale of one to five. "If you got five, you'd had a really good game. If you got one, you were wearing the correct attire. The Somerset captain of the day gave me a one once. I must have upset him."

There's an obvious question to ask. "Why did you stop umpiring?" "Because the Kwik Cricket initiative came in, which was to flood the country at primary school level with plastic cricket equipment as an introduction to boys and girls, and I was pulled out of umpiring by the Test and County Cricket Board (TCCB) at the time to front it. Which I did. And that allowed more free time for broadcasting. My first gig was with Peter Baxter at the Lord's final of the NatWest Trophy in 1986. I was the Lancashire expert, and John Barclay was the Sussex one. We were broadcasting from the main pavilion right on the top deck. It was great. And I always remember I turned up in a very nice suit for radio, but I must have created a good impression, because I kept getting asked to do more." This was the perfect role for someone with David's knowledge and linguistic fluency. It wasn't long before he got offered a role on *Test Match Special*. "It was an absolutely vintage time, top-notch broadcasting. We had Brian Johnston leading the charge, Christopher Martin-Jenkins, Henry Blofeld, Don Mosey, the 'bearded wonder' Bill Frindall, Trevor Bailey, Fred Trueman and, just starting, a very young Jonathan Agnew."

David isn't wrong. TMS was vintage then, but times were changing at a pace, and it wasn't long before his head was turned by the new kid on the block. "In 1991 satellite TV appeared. And they approached me and, you know, it was really good money. I jumped ship and my first gig was with British Satellite Broadcasting (BSB). Sky had a dish and BSB had a 'squarial'. BSB very quickly got swallowed up by Sky, and a number of people moved across. I sort of drifted off as I got more into coaching then."

David certainly wasn't a man to rest on his laurels. In 1993 he was appointed coach of Lancashire. "We had a crack outfit in the '90s, and we worked hard on fitness and fielding. That was always my sort of mantra. You know, we might not be the best batters or the best bowlers, but we're going to outfield them. I'd have to say that that Lancashire side played hard, and they worked hard." It's here where the various cricketing roles that he has engaged in seem to make the most sense in his career path. "The biggest asset to coming back to what you know was that I'd spent time away from Lancashire, doing all sorts of other things. I considered it to be a proper job. And I'm not saying I was all powerful, but I had a bit of influence with the team captain, Mike Watkinson, working alongside him." He laughs here, he's always got a story, and he's excellent at telling them. "When I say it's a proper job, I needed somewhere to work, so they converted the gents toilets at the back of the pavilion into an office. They blocked up the urinals and put a desk and a telephone in. Absolutely brilliant it was. It was the ultimate boot-room."

David worked well with the captain and hard with the overseas players, prominent among them Wasim Akram. As a coach, he was always disciplined and valued routine. "I'd get in there at 7:30 with Mike Watkinson, who was quite an early bird as well. I'd do a couple of phone-calls, check up on the Second XI and then proceed to pick the team." David is quick to praise the people he works with, and equally effusive about the people he likes, whether cleaner, captain or chief executive. The dressing-room attendant at Old Trafford receives special mention. "He was an absolute gem called Ron Spriggs, and he would do everything for the lads, you know, brew up and whiten the pads, clean, change this, that and the other, and he'd bring in a piping-hot mug of tea for me." I ask David if he thinks he has a rose-tinted view of his past and the people who have touched his life, but we agree that he's also pretty discerning. He can be critical in his judgments. He has too much of his mother in him not to be, and there have been quite a few occasions when he has said exactly what he thought. "You don't suffer fools, do you?" I ask him. "Oh, Christ no, no, no, no! They get short shrift. And I don't ever forget." I can believe that. His memory is as sharp as a knife, especially outside of the changing-room.

David continued as coach for Lancashire until, in 1996, he was asked to take on the role for England. "Raymond Illingworth was the coach at the time, and Michael Atherton was the captain. I got a call from Athers saying, 'Look, we need to get you involved.' Raymond was happy to relinquish the coaching side of his role, remaining as Chairman of Selectors. I was to run the team, and it worked pretty well. I saw my job as being there to assist the captain. It's his team, and he runs the show. I'll clear the decks for him. I'll organise practice. I'll give him the opposition team's strengths and weaknesses. We had three-minute video cameos made of all our players doing fabulously well. This was on a VHS, and they'd take it home and show the family. I'd also have VHS shots of the opposition doing rubbish." "It was a positive approach then?" I smile at him. "Yeah, it's like, 'This is Sachin Tendulkar, look, he nicks off every two minutes, he's rubbish.'" This is David as Bumble, and he's absolutely engaging, funny and smart. There have been many occasions when talking to him has reminded me of listening to him in the commentary box, and this one today feels golden.

David worked well with Mike Atherton, Alec Stewart and Adam Hollioake, and was instrumental in creating a more robust support structure for the England team, including getting in a fitness consultant, specialist coaches and a media-relations officer to help deal with the press. He was successful in his first year with Test victories against India, New Zealand and South Africa and ODI games against India, Pakistan and the West Indies. Not known for his subtleties, and never devious, he upset Zimbabwe when he claimed that 'we murdered them and they know it' after the first Test had ended with scores level.

This was the firebrand trait that David claims to have inherited from his mother, and it wasn't the last time that he'd find himself in trouble for speaking his mind. After a 3-2 loss in the 1997 Ashes at home and a defeat away to the West Indies, David's contract was extended to 1998, and England were back to winning ways with a 2-1 victory at home against South Africa. Then, famously, he upset the Sri Lanka Cricket Board as well as the ECB, after England's tour of Sri Lanka when talking about Muttiah Muralitharan bowling he said in an interview with Simon Hughes, 'If it's legal we should be teaching it.' This wasn't straightforwardly a case of ill-judged outspokenness. Magnificent as Murali was, questions about his bowling action remain. But David's language lacked the restraint of MCC diplomacy and, at the end of 1999, after a disappointing performance by England in the home World Cup, he was released. "Yeah, I got sacked by Lord MacLaurin, and he's a lovely chap. It's the nicest sacking I've ever had." David laughs. He's as brutally honest with himself as he is with some others. Lord MacLaurin himself was quick to praise David on the innovations he'd brought in, and England have since built on the foundations that he laid. It was an important time in the rebuilding of England's cricket, and David's was a significant contribution.

He wasn't twiddling his thumbs for long, and this is testament to the high regard he was held in. "Ten minutes after the news was leaked that I was leaving, I got a call from John Gaylord, Head of Sky Cricket. He was a real rough, abrasive Australian. He said, 'You're coming to work for us. There'll be a media announcement that you're leaving, and we will jump on that ten minutes after and tell them that you're with us.' I didn't have any time to discuss whatever terms there were. And I worked for Sky for twenty-odd years."

David says that he loved commentating for Sky. For many viewers, it seemed a match made in heaven. David and his 'start the car' commentary has always been popular, lively and engaging. He was always encouraged to take risks and be himself, he tells me.

Indeed, the T20 Blast Finals Day has never been the same since the loss of his infectious laughter, and his inimitable commentary on the mascot-race has been sorely missed. In an interview with Mel Farrell in *Wisden Cricket Monthly*, David is quoted as saying, 'I'm going to say this: I think the Blast needs me. I've listened to them, and they're doing fine, but there's something missing, and I could provide that something.' He's not wrong. Losing his job at Sky (shortly after he was named by Azeem Rafiq in a DCMS Parliamentary select committee hearing relating to his experience of racism at Yorkshire CCC) is still a source of bitterness, and although David insists, "I won't forget," he's aware that broadcasting has changed and there is no longer room for misinterpretation. But there's no doubt that he's still in huge demand. He knows the game inside out, has lived it boy to man and has experienced it in many different guises. He is also uncommonly good at commentating – and that hasn't changed. He still does the Lancashire games on the BBC and on livestream, and he's an extremely popular speaker at events up and down the country.

"And so just to sum up very quickly, cricket has been your life, really, hasn't it?" I ask. "It has, and it's been a bloody good life as well. And, you know, I'm very comfortably off. I'm alright. I've enjoyed myself. I've cocked up a bit, but I think everybody does." David is a complete cricketer, a talented sportsman who has made his way through his career with dedication and that unique Bumble spark that certainly isn't going to fade yet a while. A young lad from Accrington has drunk his milk. He's had pint after pint and found his fame in cricket.

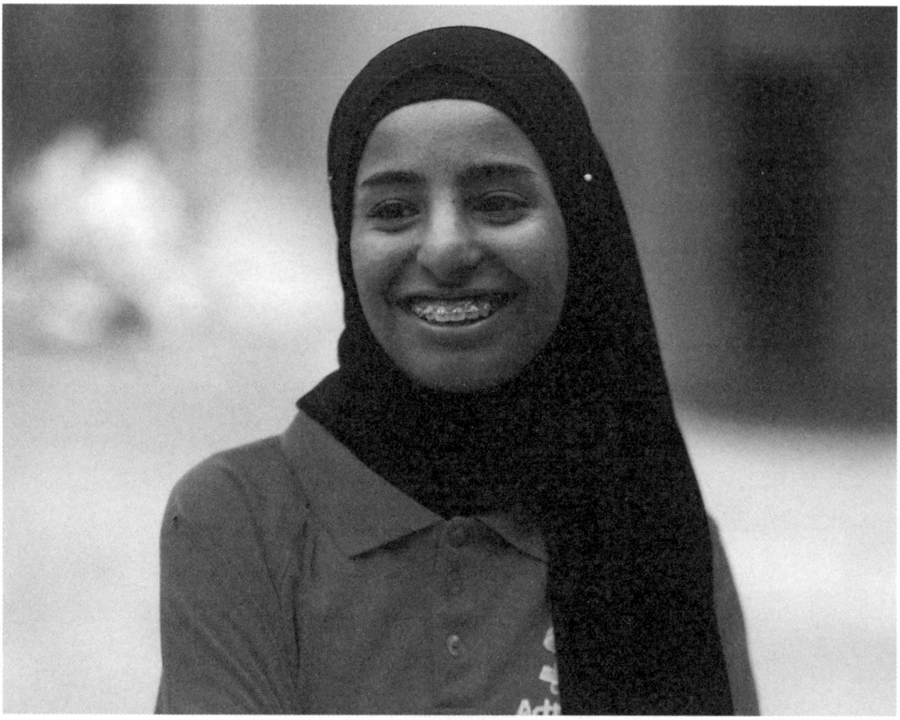

FOUNDATION
Alsama
CRICKET

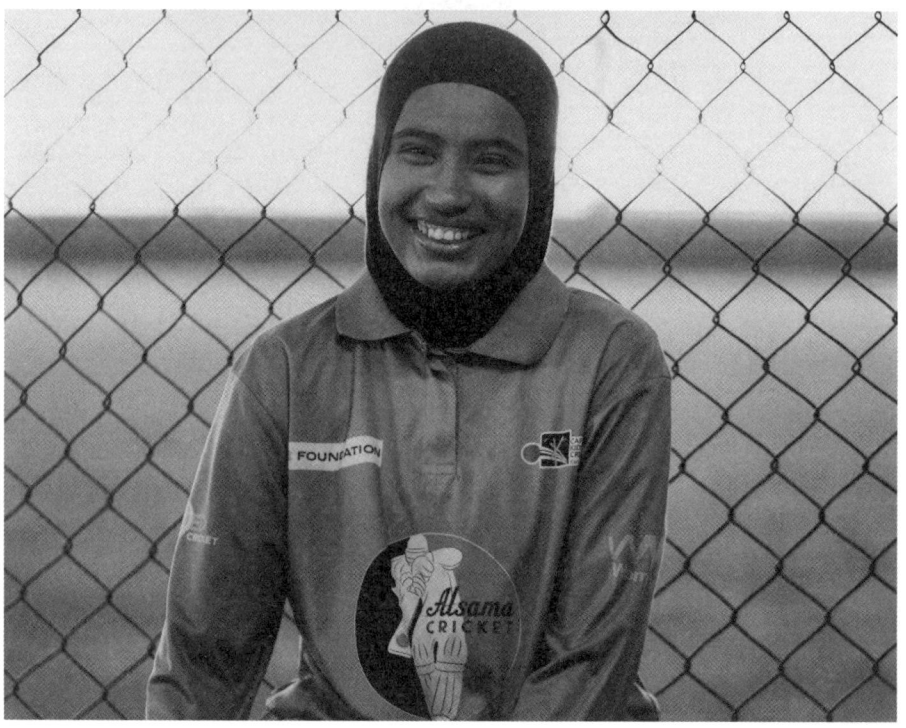

Wissal Al-Jaber and Maram Al-Khodir

IN THE WAR-TORN STREETS of Deir ez-Zor in eastern Syria, besieged by ISIS militants, Wissal Al-Jaber (bottom) suffered atrocities that are way beyond my imagination. After witnessing the beheading of her aunt, Wissal remained imprisoned in her home for over a year, fearing for her life. Meanwhile, Maram Al-Khodir (top) was subjected to appalling experiences as numerous as they are horrific.

Without theatrics Wissal vividly describes to me the barely believable. How the very act of stepping over decapitated bodies as she made her way through the centre of her home town became commonplace. When the danger of remaining in their home began to increase, both girls had little choice but to escape with those in their family who were able to travel. Leaving the terrible violence behind they headed off to face new dangers and an unknown destination. On reaching a new country, they had to make important adjustments battling against the constraints of societal conventions in order to make a life for themselves. Even in relative peace, their fight for freedom was not straightforward. It was over cricket that they met, bonded and carved out a previously unimaginable future.

I find it astonishing that I am able to communicate with these girls from their home in a refugee camp in Lebanon. It is a privilege to listen to what they have to say as I interview the two of them together on Zoom. Hoping it will prove possible to feature one of their stories it soon becomes very clear that they are a pair: their lives so entwined, their past so horrific. The kind-eyed Wissal is quieter, Maram more vivacious, captivatingly energetic. Together they tell a story which is terrible and uplifting. It was fortune, rather than design, that brought them to an NGO initiative called the Alsama Project.

Wissal and Maram are among 40,000 refugees housed at the Shatila camp in south Beirut. The camp, initially planned for 3,000, is full to bursting with Syrian as well as Palestinian and Bangladeshi refugees. Both girls live in two-roomed houses which they share with some 20 others. But this isn't a hardship for them, it is a refuge. It's far from ideal, of course, and the area is well known for drug-running, one that is considered too risky to operate in by many charities and aid organisations.

The Alsama NGO was founded by Richard Verity and his wife Meike Ziervogel in 2020. They're a hugely impressive couple, who left their very comfortable lifestyle in England to 'make a difference' and it's impossible not to be impressed by their story. Richard, who is responsible for fund-raising, is well-practiced at painting the picture. I interviewed him a few weeks before I talked with the girls in order to hear about the project, discover its aims and get an idea of how cricket has influenced the lives of so many refugees.

"In 2017, Meike and I had a simultaneous midlife crisis. We both felt very dissatisfied with our outwardly very privileged and happy existences. She was a writer, had written five novels and was running a publishing company in north London. And I was doing management consultancy, spending a lot of time in company headquarters, airports and hotels. What was clearly missing from our lives was any kind of social impact. The moment our children left us for university, we had this opportunity to do something about that sense of dissatisfaction. So we went off to Lebanon, me to be the temporary CEO of another NGO and Meike, who speaks fluent Arabic, to work on one of the programmes inside that NGO and to run an embroidery workshop."

Once in post, Richard tells me, he became frustrated by the norms of the NGO world. At the end of the year, he and Meike were relieved to have lived out their adventure, but happy to get back to their north London life. "But we hadn't counted on something," he tells me. "I'd done one brilliant thing. I spoke no Arabic at that stage, so I needed to find something I could do with these teenagers that didn't involve language. And that, of course, was cricket. I had been a moderate but enthusiastic cricketer most of my life, but it achieved a new importance in Shatila, as it was the only way I could connect with these kids, and connect very successfully because it became increasingly clear that they just loved it."

It's a heart-warming thought that in one of the most unlikely and unforgiving playing fields – a Lebanese refugee camp – cricket was weaving its magic. Richard is conscious, of course, of the 'do-gooder' label, of the sense of spreading the empire across the globe by foisting western values and dreams onto a fragile community.

"It might sound as if Meike and I were trying to impose goodness on an unsuspecting population but it's quite the reverse. They were desperate for more. We have been drawn further and further into this refugee camp. At the end of that year, I had forty children playing."

The enthusiasm for cricket was contagious, Richard explains, and his own obvious delight is indeed infectious. Both girls and boys found that the game released them from the confines of their lives. This escape from the crushing conditions of camp life is extremely important in instilling in them a sense of self-worth. Richard says that after a while twenty of the girls asked for empowerment classes, "which is really a fancy name for a kind of mentoring, and giving them a sense of their own worth and the courage to say no to early marriage, which is what twelve- and thirteen-year-olds are threatened with."

These empowerment classes have been extremely important to both Wissal and Maram. One of the things both girls say is that when they arrived at the camp, they had no sense of a future. When I ask them about the classes, Maram is bursting to tell me. "I remember, the woman responsible for child protection entered the playground when we were playing cricket and she told us to gather around her in a circle. She asked two questions, which were a shock for us all." The first, she explains was that she wanted to know what their dreams were. "We were so confused," Maram laughs, "we were all looking around wondering what she meant and wondered why she was asking us what we dreamt about when we go to sleep." I laugh along with the girls, but it's a heart-wrenching thought that the idea of ambition was so foreign as to be unintelligible to the children there. I question them about this, asking whether they really misunderstood, and they both nod in unison. It's a concept that they are both very familiar with now. The second question was even more poignant. "She asked us 'Who will rebuild Syria?'" Wissal explains, "We were confused and then we answered, 'There are lots of important people there. The government. They will build cities,' and she said, 'No. You are the new generation. You will do this. I trust you and I believe in you. You will do this great thing by starting in education with us.'"

And so, with the primary aim of providing a solid education and a sense of empowerment to mostly illiterate refugee children, and feeding off the hope that sprung from a waste-ground cricket pitch, the Alsama Project began. "It became clear," Richard clarifies, "that what these teenagers needed was school. They couldn't read or write their own language and they certainly couldn't read, write or speak English; they couldn't add or take away and didn't even know how to write numbers. They were clever children; they just hadn't been given the opportunity." So Alsama started to create schools, he tells me, as though that's the most natural thing in the world. But they weren't just schools, he reiterates, they were 'education hubs'. The children were going to have to work hard to make up for the time they'd already lost, and they had to work long hours, but their appetite for learning was insatiable, their work ethic extraordinary.

"Our terms last 44 weeks a year. We have barely any holidays, and then we play cricket with them pretty much every week and weekend of the year too. So we're now beginning to engage with these children seven days a week most of the year. Well, that's when you can start really transforming a child. And these children don't need much invitation because there's very little happening in their lives. They view school as an extraordinary privilege." It's an incredibly impressive and very ambitious project and, after four years, Alsama now teach Arabic, English, Maths, IT and coding skills, but most of all they teach self-respect and girls' empowerment.

When I quiz the girls about what it feels like to go to school, their eyes light up. "I remember the first time that I used paper was in creative writing. Miss Meike brought us in a painting by Pablo Picasso and asked us to write what we saw. I had no idea how to express my feelings. I just drew some things on the paper," Wissal tells me, a smile on her face. Maram adds, "She said, you must write what you are seeing in this picture. And then we told her that we didn't know how to read and write. You know, at that time we didn't know how to say we are illiterate. We didn't know how to communicate, but she was really patient and kind with us."

They both speak English so well now that it's hard to believe that a few years ago they knew so little. What is perhaps most extraordinary is that the force behind this incredible change, Alsama, has its roots in cricket. Although I understood the reasoning behind Richard's decision to teach cricket in such an unlikely environment, I want to know more about how it evolved, and why he thought it had been so immediately successful.

"I knew how much I loved cricket. But I hadn't quite realised what a mystical, powerful sport it can be. It teaches success and failure, which is incredibly important. To start with, the kids can't take it, and they get angry when they fail. They've had too much pain in their lives. They haven't realised that success and failure are both constrained, and that the failure is part of the enjoyment. The success will come in its own time. Also, critically, cricket teaches leadership for girls. You can't give leadership roles in the classroom terribly easily, but on the cricket pitch, it's straightforward. Just make them captain, or make them coach." And that's one of the things that they have really focused on for the last couple of years, Richard tells me. They have expanded their schools to four, which means 880 children are now receiving full-time education. Of that number, they have around 600 playing cricket, and many of the original pupils have been given coaching positions.

The leadership opportunities and team-building skills inherent in cricket are clearly described by Richard, and when I ask Wissal and Maram about their views and roles in cricket, it exactly matches what Richard has said. Their pride and their love of the game are so evident. Maram was given the role of coach and is quick to tell me she has done well at it: "I am a cricket coach and a young ambassador for MCC. I've been chosen to be an ambassador for a day by the British Embassy here in Lebanon." If anyone can sell the game to the world, believe me, it is Maram, and I tell her this. It is their way of giving back to Alsama, Wissal explains, helping others enjoy cricket as much as they have. "Now it's our turn to teach the new generations. That's the idea. That's what we are working on, what our vision is. We love cricket, we love to coach cricket. We want everyone in the Middle East to love it, too."

It's the next question that really hits the mark. If I could capture a look and keep it with me forever, then this is one I'd hold on to. When I ask Maram, "Why is cricket so special?" she positively punches the air and sets off at pace about the merits of cricket. "Oh, this is an amazing question. So you are asking why cricket? Why not another sport? Well, first of all, cricket includes boys and girls together. This is really important for us because, as you know, people in the Middle East believe in males more than females. If you can play something like this or anything that embodies these two genders together, you will love it. So this is first reason. The second? It doesn't just rely on strength but on mental, and this is amazing for the girls. For us, for example, we don't have lots of strength, but we have sometimes won against the boys because we use our mentals and they use their strength, so it's really amazing."

And Wissal, calmer in her response but no less emphatic, explains, "I think there is something really special in the cricket they are teaching us here in Lebanon. What they are doing is building girls' and boys' personalities. As a child, I was really shy, but cricket has helped me to learn to speak up. They are making us leaders by giving us abilities." Wissal goes on to explain that when she had been playing for a little while, Mohammed Khier, Alsama's Palestinian-Syrian head cricket coach, decided to make her a captain of the girls' team because he believed that she had a strong personality. He felt that her strength meant that she would be able to share the skills that she learned from cricket with the others and benefit the society around her. "So, for my girls' team, if I have any information related to cricket, I tell them about it. I ensure that they aren't stressed, it's a very nice relationship between coaches and players and everyone in the playground. There's love." But there's more than love and respect, and we discuss the sense of freedom in this teamwork, something they've never before shared. Both girls recite to me the Alsama principles: Commitment, Collaboration and Ambition. It's well-rehearsed, but it is heartfelt.

Richard has nothing but praise for Wissal. "She is very good at writing and has won a poetry competition. She is also a very knowledgeable cricketer and an impressive off-spinner, and although she isn't fast so she isn't necessarily a natural fielder, she has excelled at being a very patient coach." They have been so impressed by the application and knowledge of some of the children-turned-coaches that now only four of their thirty coaches are adults. The remaining ones are students who have had up to four years' cricket. Richard assures me that they are far more skilful than the adults and actually very good at coaching.

When I speak to Richard about the ability of the players and how seriously they take learning the art of the game, he answers unequivocally, "We're aiming for excellence here. We're not fooling around. This is not just enjoyment. The aim is to become the best possible cricketer you can." Richard and Meike have brought with them to Alsama a real essence of the ambition that has driven them in their own careers. This isn't something done just for the sake of it – the two of them know that there is little point in the help they give if it is half-hearted. There are many possible outcomes of the cricket training, body awareness and a better understanding of competition among them. But these are not the primary drivers. The game is not introduced to pupils merely as something that builds character or improves physical fitness, and certainly not as nothing but fun. "What we lead with, and what gets them excited, is that we are wanting to create a world-class cricket team, a team that will beat other international cricket teams when they visit us, or if we ever get out of the country. And we are training them up to be as good as they can possibly be. We tell them that we want them to be excellent, and as soon as we say that, then suddenly they come alive."

With my conversation with Richard in mind, I'm interested in how Wissal and Maram feel about their cricket, and in how they started to master the game. "I mean, it's not a natural sport," I suggest. "Did it take you a long time to understand it and get better?" "Of course, yes, we found it hard," says Maram. "First of all, it was a totally new game for us all. The coaches had no idea about cricket. So we were learning, and they were learning and teaching us at the same time. But we also had volunteers who came to teach the coaches, so that they could teach us in turn. I found bowling was really hard to start with, because you have to keep your arm straight and bounce the ball. But I learned how to keep it straight and focus on length and so I developed."

It's a very structured system, I soon learn. There are set levels – beginner, competent, competitive, advanced, International Professional (IP) and, the absolute elite, International Professional Plus (IP Plus). The children work their way up the levels, some becoming coaches and some formidable players. Wissal, now a seasoned coach, has a natural empathy for the beginners, and perhaps that's why she was singled out so quickly as a coach.

"When we start with the beginner team, I can tell you that it's very hard for them to play with a straight arm, or to throw a ball to the wicket, or to hit a good shot. They find it tough to learn and they have difficulty concentrating. They just want to have fun and meet friends. But then, after six months of training, they start to love and understand the game more, and then they work on their own skills, improving so they move to a higher level." "And eventually they arrive at IP Plus, where we are!" interrupts Maram, unable to remain silent at this. "We are the highest group and we will participate in the Olympics in 2028!" And yes, I'd be enthusiastic too. What a contrast to the turmoil of a few years before. An incredible ambition that couldn't be further from their struggles in their past life.

In the context of this stark contrast, I ask them whether cricket has helped them to leave those nightmares behind. "When you got to the camp and you started playing cricket, did you find that it took you away from all the horrors that you'd seen?" It isn't as simple as that, Maram explains. Cricket didn't just happen for her, she had to fight to play it.

"My family were really closed. They just wanted me to sit at home, wear long clothes, not to chat with boys. Don't do this. Don't do that. I felt like a butterfly that couldn't fly. But then, when I entered the playground, I didn't feel like this. I could move between flowers and felt free to play, to love, to dance, to sing, to do whatever. During the game I'm singing and I'm dancing, because I find it is a great chance to express myself, and that's what Alsama cricket is giving me." For Maram, it was a huge escape to be outside with other people of her own age. At first, the cricket was incidental, but the relationship with the coaches and players was key to her growth and her sense of self-worth. To succeed, there needed to be a focus, a goal and a sense of community – all part of the escape from the constrictions that her life had forced on her. "The coaches were incredible," she explains, "because they gave us the space to express, to feel life, to forget all the family issues, the war, all the bad situations that we saw back there. To escape everything. When I entered the playground, I felt like I could live. When I hit the ball, it helps with everything inside me. Anger, pressure, stress, everything. The ball can fly, and so can I."

Wissal agrees, if somewhat less demonstratively, but in addition to what Maram says, she relates her experience from the standpoint of a coach. "When I see the smile on the faces of my players, I really adore this moment. I feel like I'm the only hope for them to really build themselves, to really start to think about their futures. That way we can achieve our dreams. We understand the players because they have come from difficult backgrounds as well." Both girls explain that they are able to support all the others because they can identify with them and understand their concerns. "We give them love and the same space that our coaches gave to us. Space to express themselves, to play and to do what they want. Because cricket is a chance for everyone to get a feeling for life."

Without really knowing the area and its restrictions, it's hard to get a sense of how many competitive cricket games they get to play, but when I ask Richard he explains that, through Alsama, cricket has reached out to other areas, and there are games between Shatila, Bourj el-Barajneh and Beqaa Valley. Richard has also received generous funding from the MCC Foundation and other charitable organisations, which means that international and Olympic cricket could one day become a reality.

It's hard to quantify the effect that cricket has had on the children when you look at the Alsama project as a whole. The impact of the schooling must surely be paramount, but the whole thing began with a game that, to Richard, encompassed all the fundamental life skills that the children were starved of and which were necessary for their growth. When I question him about this, he has a fascinating answer.

When his wife, who knows nothing about cricket, enters the school room, she can immediately recognise those who have been playing cricket. "The ones that have been part of the cricket team show an understanding of structure, and they are quiet. They understand order and what it means to be in a classroom. Those who haven't had that experience are quite wild and are harder to control."

"What future do the children realistically have?" I ask Richard. Leaving little to doubt in his response, Richard stresses the huge difference that the Alsama Project has made to the lives of so many. It is offering them a lifeline, and that's a huge deal. "There are very powerful reasons to want to be a coach," Richard says. For one thing, coaches are paid a small wage of around $80 a month. "It's child labour of the best kind," he tells me. "It's enough to pay the rent on a house in Shatila, and that really matters." What it does is stop parents from withdrawing their children from the project. The regular options for Syrian refugees are either picking up rubbish in the street, building or marriage. The wages from the cricket coaching support some of the older children who are under threat of losing their new-found independence. Richard explains that they are also firm about encouraging the children to look at what they want to achieve. The rate of early marriage in Syrian refugees amongst girls is around 41% for thirteen- or fourteen-year-olds." He is proud to claim that the project has lost only one of its 880 children to marriage. "So, we can make a dramatic difference to their life simply by giving them education and incentives to stay in education."

Wissal and Maram are living proof of this. Through the screen on my Zoom call, both girls ooze confidence and a genuine pride in what they've achieved. As they stare back down the camera at me, truly another world in a lens, they are not victims, they are survivors. It's obvious that they feel cricket has been a major part in their development, and a vital focus for their future. For the present, they tell me, they are busy planning for the Olympics. "We have a strategy. You know, it's a plan. We are preparing a boys' team and a girls' team for LA 2028."

Daniel Norcross

THERE'S AN ELEMENT of the extrovert about Dan Norcross. Loosely strung together by cigarettes and fine wine, he has an encyclopaedic knowledge of cricket and a generosity of spirit that immediately puts you at ease. On a cold January evening we sit outside the Wheatsheaf opposite Tooting Bec tube. He fidgets with his case of roll-ups as we mitigate the freezing temperature with a blast from a planet-sapping patio heater. Holding court, he describes his childhood as 'rambunctious', a word that conjures up for me a home full of personality. It's clearly left its mark on Dan.

In a roundabout way, his route into cricket helped me with mine. Without the drive and vision that led him to form *Test Match Sofa*, I would never have been recruited by its offspring, *Guerilla Cricket*, and I wouldn't have forged so many links in the cricket world. In short, I wouldn't have had a launch-pad to enable me to express my love of the long-format game, nor been taken up by the BBC. I'm one of many that Dan has paved the way for, and so his cricket journey is inextricably linked to mine; he founded a team and I'm a tailender.

Dan is a bit of a maverick, in that he doesn't always listen to the accepted view, but he also has the bravery to challenge orthodoxy. In addition, he has contacts in every pocket of cricket, in business, law and finance, and in life, from quiz-machine junkies to the inhabitants of Bohemian bolt-holes. I'd call him the Oliver Cromwell of cricket journalism, but I don't think he'd put his success down to divine providence. I doubt there's a pious bone in his body. Every time I've met him he's been convivial, generous with his time and reassuringly flamboyant. He may have a slight look of Alec Guinness' George Smiley about him, but he certainly doesn't resemble him in personality. He's altogether too outgoing to make a great spy.

I could sit and talk with Dan all evening about the current cricket climate, but I'm there to find out about him so, with a bottle of wine between us, I ask him to tell me about himself. "I was born about one and a half miles from where we're sitting. I'm a very adventurous man," he starts. "I was born in Clapham South – at home, because my mother was very traditional like that. She was a very unusual woman and used to show me, in a very macabre way, the exact spot on the floorboards where the afterbirth spewed out. Every birthday it was like, 'Do we have to go through this bloody charade again?'" "What year was that?" I ask him, keen to move on from the image. "1969. It was a very full house. I had three older siblings, two much older brothers and a sister. I was repeatedly reminded that I was a mistake. There'd been terminations before me, but the Terminator was unwilling to perform a third time. He just said, 'Look, you know, just make contraception work. I'm buggered if I'm doing that again.' So, I got spared the knife by pure chance. But yes, it was a highly political, very argumentative and lively house." "Left-leaning?" I ask, knowing Dan's own politics. "Oh God, now there's a question! My dad was quite a big noise in the Communist Party in the 1950s and 60s. He left school at fourteen and fought for the Navy during the war from the age of fifteen, because you could in those days. He came out of that intensely politicised, as a lot of people did after their experiences of fighting and being told what to do by Etonians and Oxbridge types. And then he became a union man and a printer. He eventually educated himself in his late twenties." Dan is a fabulous raconteur, and he creates a vivid picture of the discussions they must have had around the dinner table. "Did he get a formal education?" I ask. "Yes, he went to Ruskin College, which was a trade-unionist college at Oxford. And then he went to Leeds University to study English, where he met my mother, who was an immensely petit-bourgeois daughter of a grocer in Yorkshire. You couldn't really have imagined two more different backgrounds."

Dan explains that his parents had a child out of wedlock and then got married. He [Dan's father] was ten years older than her. It sounds so brilliantly sixties, this bohemian lifestyle. "In what way was your childhood political?" I ask. "Well, it started when I was very little, in the 1974 election. Our dining room was a Labour Party committee room, and in 1979 it was a Tory party committee room." This wasn't what I was expecting. "Yeah, it's a very strange thing that happened, and it's one that you see mirrored quite a lot in people who didn't have a formal education. He became a teacher, then became a deputy head at a very political school called Highbury Grove in north London (now City of London Academy, Highbury Grove). The headmaster was a man called Rhodes Boyson, who was a big Tory maniac and firebrand, a Welsh sort of Baptist. My dad believed very firmly in working-class children's education."

Dan goes on to explain that his dad felt that the ruling classes had snapped up all the best parts of education so when he taught at the comprehensive, he'd teach them all Chaucer to keep them on a par with the private schools. It's a commendable thing to do, in my view. "What changed?" I ask. "Well, his political change came about because of that weird, slightly cognitively dissonant way that people like that can go once your life became more comfortable. He found himself being messianic about teaching working-class kids, then he saw the Labour Party as middle-class liberal metropolitan elitists who didn't understand anything."

I know what Dan means to some extent. There seems to be only so far that highly politicised people can lean, and when the side you are leaning towards lets you down, you try the other. It's extremism at its strangest, but I suppose it's also a form of truth-seeking. "I guess it gave me a good grounding for when I hear all of this bullshit again," Dan says. "I understood where my dad was coming from, and I thought his motives for his beliefs were strong. But as I got older, we fundamentally disagreed on who was best placed to serve the interests of the people. But you know, we always managed to put all our differences aside the moment the cricket came on, because that was the one thing that could stop all arguments between us." "Cricket, the bedrock of a good relationship." I chuckle, because, again and again, that proves to be the case.

"The rest of your family as well?" I ask. "Not so much, no. My mother was from Yorkshire, so her dad was – I say it as though it's inevitable but it kind of is – mad on cricket. He bought me my first cricket bat when I was eight." "Was it any good?" I ask him, and with tongue firmly in cheek he replies, "No, it was rubbish. It was too big for me, but he was a Yorkshireman, so you know you don't get the right size as you'll grow into it."

Dan explains that his mother's side were from a cricket background, but that his mother didn't approve of professional sport at all. "She thought that all sportsmen and women should be unpaid and amateur. She used to leave a Jane Austen by my bedside when I was eight, and my granddad, her father, would swap it for a *Wisden* from the 1950s. I was a Surrey fan, so he bought me the 1958 edition and you can imagine what I preferred reading! I wanted to find out about Lock, Loader, Laker, Bedser, about a million wickets. It was actually very good of my grandad giving me a Surrey title-winning year, considering he was a Yorkshire fan."

Cricket was exciting in the seventies. After a bruising Ashes series in Australia in 1974/75, England had to face a fiery West Indian side in the blistering heat of the UK summer of 1976. If you were going to be intoxicated by cricket, then there wasn't a better time for it to happen. I can attest to that, but to Dan it meant even more. "I became kind of obsessed, Annie. I can't remember my life when it wasn't the single most important thing to me. I was seven, and I was so enmeshed in the West Indies series that I can't remember anything else. I've got old dice-cricket books when I'm already playing it, you know, making my own team. And I went to The Oval to watch the back end of Dennis Amiss's 200 and Michael Holding running in to bowl. I was spellbound. I went with my dad and my oldest brother, who wasn't interested in it, but he was seventeen and my dad wanted to get him out of the house. He just kept going up and getting a drink and coming back and getting increasingly pissed. I didn't move, which is partly why I get intensely irritated by people who say that kids don't have a decent attention span." He's hit the target with me, and for a while we discuss this false premise in some excitement, both of us recapturing childhoods consumed by cricket.

We return to the splendour of the 1976 series because, to both of us, it was an unforgettable rite of passage. Dan describes the feeling well. "It caught my imagination. I remember just how slowly time went by on the Saturday morning, waiting for the start, and I remember rushing out of primary school to get home to turn it on the television. Seeing Viv go berserk, the athletic magnificence of the West Indians, and the decrepitude of the English." "Yes, you were supporting England, but at the same time you were bewitched by the West Indians, and the contrast of the two teams," I say in agreement. "You know, I was a Londoner, and Brixton's not far. There were lots of West Indians, and they were engaged in the cricket and there was great excitement, so I remember it vividly, how I completely got the cricket bug, even though my mother found it the thief of time. She hated the fact that summers would pass by with the curtains closed." "Did you go outside to play at all?" I ask. "Oh yeah, we were often outdoors because we lived between two commons and went from one to the other, then in the backyard with my brothers." "Were you any good at cricket?" I ask as I don't know about Dan the cricketer. His answer makes absolute sense: "I was good enough to be able to play and really enjoy it."

I ask him about school cricket, and I'm not surprised that, like mine, his primary school had no cricket option, but his secondary school was a whole different matter. "Your secondary education wasn't at the local comprehensive was it, Dan?" I tease, knowing already the path he'd taken. "No, and it was kind of indicative of my father's moral compass, if you'd call it that. My brothers and sisters were so much older than me that when they went to school it was a grammar school but by the time I went, grammar schools were a thing of the past, and Maggie [Thatcher] had turned most of them back into independent schools. So, dad's reasoning was, if I've got to pay for you to have the same education as your siblings, you get a choice of which school you go to (if you get in), so long as I pay the same. So I chose Dulwich College, because I didn't want to be at the same school as my brothers." If Dan's younger dad could see him now, I thought. Dulwich was a school that also drew in the likes of Nigel Farage – never a contact, Dan is quick to assure me. In fact, Farage was a prefect and five years his senior. The future leader of the Reform UK Party was once responsible for placing Dan in detention but that was the extent of their interactions.

Dan went to Dulwich at the age of nine. As he tells me, "They had great facilities, so I could play lots of cricket, and I was in the school team. I started as an all-rounder, as everybody should. I had quite a late puberty and, you know, quicker bowlers tended to be the ones who had their puberty earlier and so were stronger and taller. I had my spurt when I was about sixteen to eighteen, so I sort of focused more on batting as an opener. I did a little bit of off-spin and I also really loved captaining." Dan goes on to explain that he captained the Third XI when he was fifteen, then moved to captaining the Second XI. It wasn't until he went to St John's College, Oxford, though, that he began to play cricket to his heart's content.

It's here that Dan comes into his own. Oxbridge, hedonist, cricketer. "When you go to university, if you're me, you don't really do any study, so I could net every day and I could play twice a week and then, because I got better, I became captain." There are countless tales of undergraduates running headlong into liberation, with their eyes firmly open. If you can deal with the new-found freedom and emerge unscathed with something to show for it, university life is a total delight. "Partly because the odds of getting in were higher I chose a daft degree. Latin and Greek. I mean, what's that going to do for me?" But personally, and backed up by a nod of agreement from Dan, I'd place some of the responsibility for his lack of scholarly endeavour with his dad, who, Dan tells me, left him at the university with "two bottles of Thunderbird and made me promise him that I wasn't going to work too hard, and that I would throw myself into ancillary activities."

University life fitted comfortably with Dan's love of cricket. He used the nets and the adjoining bar in equal measure and claims he was a half-decent cricketer. It was when he left, he tells me, that he reverted to being 'mediocre'. He blames the difficulty of travelling in London for forcing him to cut back to playing or practising only twice a week. I interpret this as a confession that he needed to have the facilities easily available, but I may be being unfair. "So you came back to London after university?" I surmise. "Yes, straight back and lived in the flat that I'm still in now." "It's quite a big flat then?" I ask. "Yes. It was bought by my parents. My dad retired when I was eighteen, and my mum retired the moment I left university. They had a large town house in Clapham, which you could buy in those days, even if you were teachers. Completely impossible now. In 1986, they sold it and bought a cottage in Warwickshire as well as the flat. The idea was that they would spend every weekend in the cottage, with a view to emigrating to Warwickshire at a future date. And the point at which they moved was literally when I finished university. I came back after my finals, and there was a note on the freezer that said, 'We've gone to Warwickshire for good. There's enough food in the freezer for a week. After that you're on your own.'" It reminds me of the hero of Jan Needle's children's book, *Wagstaffe the Wind-up Boy*, whose parents run away from him. I'm sure that wasn't the case with Dan's parents, but the similarity to Wagstaffe makes me smile.

Dan left university in 1992 with a third-class degree in Classics and access to a large flat in south London. To help pay the rent he set about filling it with friends. Two spare rooms; two friends in each room. "Basically, I continued my university life with my university friends," he admits. It's a perfect scenario for any recent graduate. "It was lovely," he tells me. He began this stage of his life as what can only be described as a chancer. Calculating how to maintain a student lifestyle, he summed up his assets. Dan and his friends were good at quizzes and they were good at drinking. The early 1990s were the heyday of the pub quiz-machine. "I learnt all the answers to three quiz machines. We discovered that they had a database of around 3,000 questions, and ever since I was a boy I'd been good at remembering things. I mean, when I was nine I had a stand-up row at my grandmother's funeral with my grandfather about the relative merits of Len Hutton and Jack Hobbs in terms of the number of runs each had scored. My ability to recall facts stood me in good stead when it came to delaying the inevitable decision on what I was going to do with my life because I could literally go to three pubs a day and guarantee I could take £20 in cash out of each one." "You've probably never been better off," I laugh. "Yes. In 1993 I paid for everything in pound coins." "So what changed?" I ask, "What burst the bubble?" "Well, my story is a lot to do with computing. What happened was computers got better, and suddenly instead of 3,000 questions, there were 20,000."

It's possible to see in Dan's life an embodiment of the growth of computer science. Dan and his friends needed proper jobs, he tells me. "Computers got better, and bizarrely I got paid a lot less to work more." Dan found himself working for the former City Editor of the *Daily Express* on a project to digitalise the Press Association Library using an indexing system that made it possible to scan newspaper pages and create image files by clicking on the four corners, rather than articles having to be cut out with scissors. "Ultimately, it all got superseded by the improvement in the Internet," Dan explains. These improvements saw companies thinking up ways to 'win the Internet'. He was savvy enough to recognise that selling holidays was one of the ways forward, but the people he worked for were pipped at the post by lastminute. com who, unlike Dan's company, accepted the money offered to them by a venture-capital firm.

During this time Dan met his future wife, Catherine, via one of his many connections, this time at his best friend's workplace. Dan tells me that much of his early life was made up of a series of lucky breaks and this was one, but I think his journey has been a mixture of luck, contacts and blind optimism. Dan had been offered a project manager role because he was in the right place at the right time, but he also believed he would come good or at least wasn't afraid of the consequences. As it happened, he was probably a bit too honest and, as he explains, "I discovered something really bad, which is 'never tell the truth to bosses'. I'd been sitting there trying to work out what their business plan was, and I realised there was a big error, that basically their consultants had made an assumption that required every single one of our sales force to work for 25 hours a day for seven days a week. So I went to the board and told them that. Two weeks later they made us all redundant because their consultants had fucked up. So that taught me a lesson."

Needing a new direction and left with some redundancy money, Dan turned his hand to script-writing and produced a play, which he then turned into a film. "We filmed in my block of flats. It was called *The Tapes*, and it was basically like *My Little Eye*. The idea was that what you were watching was entirely unreliable, because it had been edited by a Peeping Tom, who'd put secret cameras throughout the house." "Was it successful?" "Yes in that it paid for itself. We made a small amount of money, but it was just brilliant to be able to do something creative." But the frustration was there. Dan didn't consider himself a real 'luvvie'. He tells me, "I was still only energised by cricket really, but I could see no way of working in it. All the jobs were taken by lifers in journalism, and all the commentary positions were taken. You know, Blowers and Christopher Martin-Jenkins had been there for thirty years, Jonathan Agnew for twelve. Then there'd be an overseas commentator. I didn't even think about cricket as an option." Just as things were getting difficult job-wise, Dan was offered a role at a company that had previously made him redundant. "I'd been really staring down the barrel, and then this opportunity helped to pay off my residual debts." "You say you were staring down the barrel. Did you get depressed?" "No, it's been a weirdly lucky thing for me. Catherine finds it a combination of enchanting and infuriating." "You kind of ride the wave?" I ask. "Well, I just ignore it. I like to put my head in the sand, and then there will be a moment I might start to feel sudden panic, but I just distract myself by a drink or watch TV and think something will turn up." "Which I suppose is a coping mechanism," I suggest. "A bit of entitlement as well, but also a willingness to say yes to things." He confirms. This is the perfect explanation as to how he's managed to do what he's done and how he went on to spectacular success, riding the waves of the 2008 dot.com bubble bursting and surfing his way right onto the cricket web.

With the unpredictability of a changing internet market, Dan was out of a job once more, but with a decent pay-off. He was determined on one thing, "What I wasn't going to do, given that the 2005 Ashes happened without me seeing any of it because I was working, was to miss the 2009 Ashes. I thought, look, I'm coming up to forty, and all I've done is firefight or try to do ridiculous things. When I tried to do something creative and artistic, I realised that it was all about contacts. If you're going to get major sitcom or film projects, then you need to know people. They don't sink money into total unknowns, and I didn't have contacts in that industry. But I did have contacts in IT, and I did have an obsessive love of cricket."

Dan tells me that he wanted to do something in cricket, and, using a combination of contacts and bluster, he came up with a template for a changing world. "I looked into running a live stream and an audio that could stand up, and although I was technically pretty inept, I wasn't illiterate, so I knew how things worked from having to manage projects. What I didn't know was the technicals. There was now a robust enough stream meaning you could definitely do this. All I needed was someone to design a website." Dan had the necessary contacts, and he reached out to them. They included Nigel Walker (The Bear) who was a member of his cricket team, and happened to be a sound engineer. The Bear came good, as did a website designer. Suddenly Dan had his website with a robust stream, microphones and a mixer. All he needed was the people and the name.

The name was given to him by a friend called Steve Busfield, Yorkshireman and mad cricket fan. "Steve said, 'It's obvious, you have to call it *Test Match Sofa*. It's about Test cricket, and you're sitting on a sofa.' The *Sofa* began on the first day of the 2009 Cardiff Ashes Test, a date that Dan remembers as "one week to the day after my mother had died during a routine operation".

His father died the January after. These shockingly sudden deaths made the *Sofa* all the more crucial to him. Absorbing himself in cricket, he could ignore the distress that these losses had caused him. Traumatic as it was, his parents' deaths provided him with a timely inheritance that he was able to invest into the *Sofa*. I'm sure they would have approved, I think, 'thief of time' or not.

"The first big thing that happened was that, after the first Test, Barney Ronay wrote a piece about us in the *Guardian* and it gave us something to point to." From fifty friends and family listening in on the first day, by the end of the Ashes they were getting a few thousand listeners. "We had to make a decision," Dan tells me. "whether we were serious about this." "Because you weren't making any money, you were just doing it for the love of the game," I interject. "Yes," he agrees. "It was all coming out of my redundancy money. I'd paid to get the website up and running, but I couldn't pay anybody anything until we got money coming in. I'd go out and buy a load of booze and some food for everyone." Despite the lack of financial reward, Dan managed to get a group of cricket enthusiasts to contribute, including livewires like Manny Cohen and Jonathan Zoob, a pensions tax expert who also happened to be a concert pianist, then later, Guerilla commentators the Bear, Gary Naylor and Nigel Henderson. "When you listen to everybody's first commentary stint, they're bad, but what I found startling was the speed with which people got really good," Dan explains.

They were making headway and headlines and had begun to attract insomniacs and people who wanted to get involved, but the game changer, Dan tells me, was discovering Twitter in 2010. They replaced the lack of crowd noise with jingles that were sometimes played live on the piano by Zoob, and they started to get a loyal following. "Who did the original jingles?" I ask. "Oh, we did them in my bedroom. They were utterly stupid, but they pleased us, and it sort of set the tone for what the programme was, which was completely alternative. It wasn't supposed to be *Test Match Special*. We were supposed to be utterly irreverent, drinking, smoking, swearing and being really angry with things when they didn't go well, and really pleased when they did." "So what happened?" I ask the million-dollar question. "Well, basically we had two years of grace, where we were getting better and better." That's when Andy Zaltzman came on, and with him came fellow comedians

Miles Jupp and Mark Steel. There were some fabulously talented people involved, and Dan even got some private investors via Henry Dimbleby, a university friend who introduced Dan to Katie Walker, who became a regular commentator. "The programme got entirely elevated because we had a large group, and we also had a roster of women, which the BBC didn't, so the sound was richer and different arguments would take place. We had music and we had comedians and we reached this absurd point when we were getting 70,000 people listening to our coverage of the 2010/2011 Ashes."

Things started to get a little out of control because, as Dan explains, they were working too much. His project manager, it seems, had gone rogue. "I did 186 days of unpaid commentary in 2011. We were getting small dollops of sponsorship, so we were able to pay our way, but I wasn't able to pay myself. I was loving it, but it was becoming increasingly impossible. Catherine had a high-powered job with London First, a business membership organisation that, among other things, lobbied the government, and I wasn't contributing aside from getting paid for the odd article."

With journalists like Elizabeth Ammon and George Dobell coming on the show and writing articles about it, and with a feature in the 2010 *Wisden*, the *Sofa* was becoming more of a three-piece suite. Exposure was leading to more exposure. The more input the more avenues, the more avenues the wider scope. "Aatif Nawaz (comedian and actor) and Henna Khan joined, so we did more Pakistan matches, and we were getting more and more polished and working through the night." Dan needed to find a way to monetise the *Sofa*.

It was, in many ways, a perfect time for development, because the *Cricketer* and *All Out Cricket* magazines were looking at ways of expanding their websites. Dan tells me, "I said to them, 'Look we give you a feed of the cricket and you can advertise, and your writers can come on and we can talk about the magazine. There's lots of good synergy here.' Then Neil Davidson, who had taken over the *Cricketer*, came in with a substantial offer." Dan went on to explain that Andrew Miller, who was working at the *Cricketer*, had been on the *Sofa* and was a huge supporter. He had persuaded Davidson that the *Sofa* was just what they needed to launch their new website, convincing him that it gave them unique content. "I met them, and we made a deal. They gave me enough money to pay everyone off who had invested in the *Sofa*, and all the people who'd helped me." On top of that, the *Cricketer* paid Dan a wage, basically to be the lead commentator, but also to put the team together and to organise the rotas.

It's a familiar story. Investment is needed, but with that money comes regulations and restrictions. "That's when things became awkward," Dan explains, "because the programme got objectively slicker. We had to be less sweary, much to my irritation because it felt like they didn't want us to be us. To be honest, I'm not sure that they quite understood what they'd bought. They didn't get that, fundamentally, no one was going to listen to us if we were trying to be *Test Match Special*, because they were doing that so much better than we ever could. I mean they were at the ground for a start."

It was more worrying than that, though, because as soon as the *Cricketer* looked to be taking the *Sofa* seriously, others began to feel threatened. "The *Cricketer* got a bit spooked," Dan admitted. "Jonathan Agnew had been on the board of the *Cricketer* and he felt, quite understandably, that this was something of a betrayal. He thought they were buying a competitor to *Test Match Special*. Partly because of this scandal, everyone started noticing that we were there." "That was a good thing," I say, part question, part statement. "Really good and really bad, because then we were dealing with the madness of sporting rights." *Sofa* was in the spotlight and suddenly they were seen as a huge threat to mainstream broadcasting. Dan goes on to tell me that, "David Collier had called me 'the most dangerous man in English cricket', because I'd got a bunch of middle-aged sweary people to shout at the TV screen to reach the parts that other broadcasts couldn't reach. We were on the Internet, so, you know, our listenership was in Thailand, Brazil etc. because we weren't geo-blocked. I thought we were just bringing the joy of cricket to the wider world, and I was really proud of that. But then it became clear that I was a scheming, terrible bastard, who was trying to undermine the basis of cricket!"

Dan admits that he could, of course, understand the perturbations, but he found that it became really unpleasant. "Christopher Martin-Jenkins, in his last article, said we were 'parasites who should be nailed down and swept off the Internet'. I don't think I helped myself by being a clever dick when interviewed about this, saying that 'as much as I have respect for CMJ, the problem is if you nail it down it's really hard to sweep it off.' I didn't realise CMJ was dying at the time."

Dan explains that he had a brilliant lawyer, yet another contact from university, a man who had sold property rights for the IPL, so he knew his stuff. "Whenever we got a letter telling us that we couldn't do this because we hadn't paid for the rights to do it, my lawyer would write and say, 'Well, I think you'll find that you're allowed to watch TV and talk about it. If you wish to change the fundamental laws of freedom of speech in the UK then feel free. While you're doing that my client will continue to do what he's doing.' This drove them mad, because they thought, 'Why don't you stop? We're huge and you're tiny.'"

It was only a matter of time. The growth couldn't continue, and although Dan refused to stop the broadcasting, he had the authorities constantly at him from one side, which meant that the *Cricketer* started to come at him from the other. It came to a peak when Andrew Miller, while working for the *Cricketer*, was frog-marched out of the press-box for tweeting about the *Sofa*, then had his press accreditation taken away. "So I can see it from the *Cricketer*'s point of view. We were no longer being very helpful, because we were denying their right of access to games. The authorities couldn't stop us, but they starved us of the oxygen of access. They told all journalists that if they went on the *Sofa* they would not get accreditation. And they went further – the *Sofa* had a deal with the *Daily Mail* to put up the *Sofa* audio player on their website. We were going to interview Lawrence Booth [editor of the *Wisden Almanack*] after play every day. He did the first day and was then told that he'd have his accreditation revoked in India if he continued."

It seems that Dan was again just a bit too forward-thinking for the world of cricket. It was still the early days of the Internet, and he was frustrated that nobody had really understood how to monetise the *Sofa*. "I guess there was so much potential, but we were too early for people whose jobs were in the 'old' world, to be able to support us, and I didn't have either the time or the contacts to man the phones. I could have explained myself better, but I don't think they were in a mood to listen, and I think it was hard for them because it was the start of a very different world and they were magazines: a hard-copy world trying to break into a digital world, and the people who can do that more easily are the ones who haven't come from that world of print in the first place."

Dan succeeded in reaching an understanding with Jonathan Agnew who assisted in forming a plan for the *Sofa*. "Jonathan was really helpful in trying to get the *Sofa* to do a watch-along programme, not ball-by-ball, but providing an alternative view for the ECB during the 2013 Ashes and beyond. I couldn't justify not doing ball-by-ball for that Ashes, but we'd agreed an exit strategy immediately afterwards – to take everybody out of the *Sofa* and go and join the ECB and do something with them." But after the disappointment of the 2013/14 Ashes there was a big re-structuring of staff at the ECB and these plans didn't materialise, Dan explains. "The whole thing was dead." But he had at least healed the rift between *Sofa* and *TMS*.

Despite a last-minute threat to pull the plug on the entire thing, Dan managed to get the Ashes series over the line. "I got everyone paid up, and then I said, 'I just can't do it anymore.'" Dan admits that he needed and wanted a work/life balance and was starting to hate his days, so he decided he needed to leave. "I'm quite weak in some ways," he explains ruefully. "I like conviviality and I like people to like me and for work to be fun. The *Sofa* was about infectious enjoyment and spreading our love of the game but also inspiring people. My mantra was always, 'This isn't my programme, anybody can do it.' Anybody who came on, I'd give them a bit of a hand and they could always talk to me after the game. We had got a place for them."

But Dan had run out of steam and felt that he had lost the confidence of his team, as questions were raised over his managing of the *Cricketer* relationship. It was time to leave them to decide if they wanted to continue the partnership. With the technical nous of the Bear and the journalistic skill of Henderson, the connection with the *Cricketer* ended and the *Sofa* morphed into *Guerilla Cricket*. Dan tells me that he's incredibly proud that *Guerilla Cricket* managed to secure the sole rights for Ireland's Test debut. "It was one of the things we'd been trying to do for ages with the *Cricketer*, to get them to buy the rights to a low-level series. For *Guerilla Cricket* to get Ireland's inaugural Test against Pakistan in

2018 was an important moment in Test history. They're part of that history now for ever."

When Dan left the *Sofa*, he sent an email to Adam Mountford, the *TMS* producer to ask whether he could commentate on a county game for the BBC. "He's never subsequently answered an email of mine so quickly. Within about three minutes he sent one back asking me what I was doing for the Surrey v Gloucestershire game at the Oval in 2014."

Dan did his first commentary stint on a county game that May. "It was great to commentate at a ground. Suddenly you've got birds, you've got flags, you've got all the things that make up the broad sweep, and it's so different. Also, the speed of exposure with the BBC was completely bizarre to me. The *Sofa* had been a proving ground where you could hold your head up high and say I can do this. I knew that I could do *TMS*. Why not? I'd spent 10,000 hours training myself."

By July he was doing a Women's Test match at Wormsley. "There weren't very many people who knew women's cricket as well as I did, because I'd done lots on the *Sofa*. It was me, Charles Dagnall, Henry Moeran, Isa Guha and Mel Farrell." It wasn't much over a year before Dan was doing his first men's ODI and his first Test the year after. "It all happened quickly, but I guess I'd spent four years doing the lead commentary. I'd had to interview people, run lunch-breaks. I had all the experience I needed." Dan recalls how bizarre it felt to suddenly be at the top of the game. "I was lying in bed filled with adrenaline, because I'd done this unbelievable thing. Wondering how on earth it had happened, how two years ago I was doing the *Sofa*, and now here I was at Old Trafford. I'd just done England against Australia, and was lying in bed thinking, 'I got away with that', and I'm reading Twitter, and it's nearly all supportive messages, mostly from people who were involved in the *Sofa*, you know, things like 'So delighted for you.' And I'm thinking, it's lovely the community having your back, and at this point I'm almost overcome with joy. I'm like, 'Norcross you're good.'

"And then I got a message that went. 'Hey, Mr Norcross, can I beg you to resign immediately? You are the worst thing that has ever been on my favourite programme, and I don't think I can stand another day with you on it.'" This of course makes us both laugh for some time, but it also reveals a key point. You put yourself on the line, and people want to push you off it. They always do.

Dan had made it to the top, despite being the worst thing on someone's favourite programme. "Look, it's fine. It's how it should be," says Dan after we discuss how no one is immune to criticism or vitriol. Why should everybody like me? The thing is, it's a very hard thing to do, because it's different from other forms of life. When I worked as a project manager, no one came up to me at the end of a day's work and said, 'You're a fucking disgrace.' And no one came up to me and said, 'You know, you managed that project damned well.' You have to take the rough with the smooth."

He then makes an interesting point, the significance of which hits me. "I probably thought that we could do the *Sofa* because I believed we were better than the people that were on the radio. And why did I think that? Probably because I didn't like somebody's commentary, and it's like an absurd arrogance. It's utterly ridiculous, but everybody's got it. We're public property. When you do *TMS*, you're curating a national treasure of a broadcast. It has always been about community, but it's one that, until the early part of the 21st century, consisted entirely of letters that were read out. No one knew anything else, because there was no e-mail, and yet everybody knew the community. Radio is way more intimate than TV. TV preaches to its community, and you sit there and soak it up, whereas on radio you go right into people's brains, because they also try to imagine who you are." "Yes, you're their eyes." "And your voice, I mean, I see this time and time again. When people meet you and they've heard your voice, they look at you in this totally different way, because they go, 'Wait a minute! This is the noise on the radio. I thought you'd look much more handsome!'"

As we finish our drinks, I eye my watch nervously. I ask, "Just finally, where do you see your future?" "As long as the listening public and my producer will take me, I want to continue to do *TMS*. It's a terrible thing to admit, but I'm finally doing what I've always wanted to do. I have no desire to do anything else, although obviously I'd love to be on *Celebrity Antiques Road Trip* with Ebony Rainford-Brent. I can't imagine a life without cricket. It matters more to me than anything else. If bad things happen, I will run away to cricket. And when good happens, it makes me love the cricket even more." "So it's the answer to everything?" I smile. "It's like life, the universe and everything. It's tomorrow's framework. I think somebody once said to me that you could create an entire national curriculum through cricket. You've got geology, you've got geography, the pitch, you've got history, you've got maths, you've got physics. It teaches you everything you need to know."

Dan loved cricket so much that he created a show, a platform. And that's what he's most proud of, that when he looks around the press box it is made up of names and faces that began their cricket path lounging on his sofa, cadging his cigarettes and quaffing his wine.

"I believe that if you love cricket, and if you shut off the noise and aren't too self-conscious about it, if you describe what you're watching and if you've listened to the radio all your life, which all of my commentators had, you will find your style. Anybody can do this, as long as they've got the environment in which to flourish and to enjoy it." That's what Dan told me, and he's not wrong. If I can do it, anyone can, I think. And is it such a terrible thing to admit that you're finally doing what you've always wanted to do? No, I don't think it is.

Acknowledgements

There is not a chance that I would have put this book together in a coherent way without the careful, constructive feedback from my dad, Peter Thomson, or the explicit corrections from my brother, Jim Thomson. They are both far better writers than I am.

I would never have even attempted to write the book if my friend and colleague, Debbie Bucella, hadn't given me the belief that I could do it in the first place. She and my sister, Kate Squire, supported me from the outset, and for that I will be eternally grateful.

My husband, Duncan Chave, has not just been a support. He's been a sounding board, a hive of information and a silent, indispensable shadow. With Fraser Chave, our son, we are three obsessive followers of cricket, always constructing, always debating.

I want to thank Vic Marks for three things. Firstly, for agreeing to write a foreword; secondly, for being the sort of friend that you can travel seven hours on a train with and never find a moment's silence; and thirdly, for calling me a writer.

If this were *Desert Island Discs* and I could choose only one person to thank above all others, then it would have to be Stephen Chalke. I sent him my first chapter on a whim, and he enjoyed it so much that he introduced me to Fairfield Books and Matt Thacker. So I found myself with a publishing deal. But Stephen did more: he offered suggestions, painstakingly read each chapter and encouraged me throughout the process. And I thank Matt and Fairfield Books for making my dream a reality.

Thanks also to the eleven (twelve, if you separate Wissal and Maram) cricketing people who have shared their stories with me. This book is my debt to them.

Finally, there are the people who have been invaluable to me in my own cricketing journey. They come in all guises and from all manner of places, united only by their love of cricket. So in no particular order, they are: all the subscribers to *County Cricket Matters*, all my friends on the county cricket circuit, the writers of *Being Outside Cricket*, my great friends at *Guerilla Cricket*, all of the Erratics (past and present) and the teams we play, Martin Weiler and Brian Carpenter (my cricket travelling friends) and my fellow *County Cricket Matters* podcasters, Dan Whiting, Sam Dalling and Harry Everett.

Acknowledgements

I have read and made us of the following books:

- Colin Babb, *1973 and Me; the England v West Indies Test Series 1973*, Hansib Publications, 2019

- Roland Butcher and Bridgette Lawrence, Rising to the Challenge, Michael Joseph, 1989

- Rachael Heyhoe Flint and Netta Rheinberg, *Fair Play – The Story of Women's Cricket*, Angus & Robertson, 1976

- Rachael Heyhoe Flint, Heyhoe! The Autobiography of Rachael Heyhoe Flint, Pelham Books, 1978

- Fred Rumsey, Sense of Humour, Sense of Justice, Fairfield Books, 2019

- Simon Sweetman, *Enid Bakewell Coalminer's Daughter*, Lives in Cricket Series, Association of Cricket Statisticians and Historians, 2018

- Netta Rheinberg, 'Enid Bakewell, 'Champion Woman Cricketer', in *Wisden Cricketers' Almanack*, 1970, pp.119-123